A Companion to
MOZART'S PIANO CONCERTOS

A Companion to
MOZART'S
PIANO CONCERTOS

By

ARTHUR HUTCHINGS

OXFORD UNIVERSITY PRESS
Oxford   New York

Oxford University Press, Great Clarendon Street, Oxford OX2 6DP
Oxford New York
Athens Auckland Bangkok Bogotá Buenos Aires Calcutta
Cape Town Chennai Dar es Salaam Delhi Florence Hong Kong Istanbul
Karachi Kuala Lumpur Madrid Melbourne Mexico City Mumbai
Nairobi Paris São Paulo Singapore Taipei Tokyo Toronto Warsaw
and associated companies in
Berlin Ibadan

Oxford is a registered trade mark of Oxford University Press

Published in the United States
by Oxford University Press Inc., New York

First edition published 1948
Second edition published 1950
Eighth corrected impression 1991
Reissued 1998

British Library Cataloguing in Publication Data
Data available

Library of Congress Cataloging in Publication Data
Hutchings, Arthur, 1906–
A companion to Mozart's piano concertos / by Arthur Hutchings.—
2nd ed., 8th corrected impression.
p. cm.
"Thematic guide to Mozart's concertos":
Includes bibliographical references and index.
Originally published: 2nd ed., 8th corrected impression. Oxford:
Oxford University Press 1991.
1. Mozart, Wolfgang Amadeus, 1756–1791. Concertos, piano,
orchestra. 2. Mozart, Wolfgang Amadeus, 1756–1791—Thematic
catalogs. 3. Concertos (Piano)—Analysis, appreciation. I. Title.
MT130.M8H8   1998   784.2.'62'092—dc21   98–39904
ISBN 0–19–816708–3

1 3 5 7 9 10 8 6 4 2

Typeset by Hope Services (Abingdon) Ltd
Printed in Great Britain
on acid-free paper by
J. W. Arrowsmiths Ltd, Bristol

FOREWORD

CLIFF EISEN

Arthur Hutchings's *Mozart's Piano Concertos*, together with Cuthbert Girdlestone's *Mozart et ses concertos pour piano* (Paris, 1939) and Donald Francis Tovey's *Essays in Musical Analysis* (London, 1936), is one of a handful of books that virtually every Mozart-lover reads at one time or another. The reason for this is not hard to find: the concertos have rarely been described so eloquently or with such obvious affection.

To be sure, some of Hutchings's history is dated: it is not the case, for example, that K.107, Mozart's concerto arrangements of three sonatas by his London friend J. C. Bach, date from 1765; as the handwriting of the autographs shows, these transcriptions date from 1771 or 1772. By the same token, none of Mozart's early concertos was written for a Salzburg 'audience' in the modern sense—musical life in the archdiocese was under the control of the court and the nobility attached to it; at best these works were by intention 'salon' music. (The only exceptions may be K.175, which Mozart played at public concerts while away from Salzburg, and K.271, the so-called 'Jeunehomme' concerto, supposed to have been written at the request of a touring French virtuosa whose identity remains a mystery even to this day.) But then, Hutchings's volume is not a history book. On the contrary, it is an appreciation of the concertos and their musical contexts: the six quartets dedicated to Haydn, the late symphonies, the operas, and the Requiem all come in for discussion here.

If there is one chapter that is a surprise it is the short but pithy conclusion, 'Mozart and the Modern Performance'. At the time Hutchings wrote *A Companion to Mozart's Piano Concertos*, 'performance', or what we now call 'performance practice', was not fashionable, especially for music after Bach. Yet many of Hutchings's observations are distinctly 'modern', among them that the keyboard and orchestra are partners, not antagonists, and that it makes little sense to employ period instruments and performing conventions but to play from anachronistic nineteenth-century editions. In Hutchings's elegant formulation, this 'is to give ourselves an interesting and jolly evening's entertainment, no more to be confused with accurate Mozart-playing than a recent and interesting reading of *Twelfth Night* by phoneticians was to be confused with "Shakespeare as he wrote it".' Whether *any* account can recapture the concertos as the composer himself might have played them is another matter altogether, although I suspect that Hutchings would have enjoyed many modern, 'historically informed', performances. In any case, Hutchings's remarks apply equally to traditional and 'modern' performances. And in this sense he is an authentic purveyor of the eighteenth-century spirit, which valued taste above all, something this book has in abundance.

Until recently, writings on the concertos were relatively few and far between. But with the ongoing 'performance practice' debate, much of it centred on these works, the concertos have become a central concern of Mozart scholarship. Perhaps the most accessible account is Robert Levin's 'Mozart's Keyboard Concertos', in *Eighteenth-Century Keyboard Music*, edited by Robert L. Marshall (New York, 1994); similarly engaging is Konrad Küster's *Mozart: A Musical Biography* (Oxford, 1996). Stimulating discussions can also be found in Charles Rosen's *The Classical Style* (New York, 1971) and in *The Mozart Companion*, edited by Donald Mitchell and H. C. Robbins Landon (London, 1956); Dennis Forman's *Mozart's Piano Concertos* (London, 1971) deals with the first movements only. As for performance practice, it is frequently instructive to see what performers themselves have to say: Robert Levin's notes to his concerto recordings are models of their kind. Some readers may also want to consult the more specialized *Mozart's Piano Concertos: Text, Context, Interpretation*, edited by Neal Zaslaw (Ann Arbor, 1996) and in particular the editor's introduction, which gives an excellent overview of historical and performance-practice problems in the concertos in general.

The Mozart Autographs and Other Authentic Sources for the Concertos

It is clear that Hutchings placed extraordinary value—and rightly so—on Mozart's concerto autographs, devoting a page to their description at the start of his book. It was a fairly easy matter, in those days, to account for them: the vast majority were owned by the Prussian State Library, Berlin. The Allied bombing of Berlin during the Second World War, however, forced the library to evacuate its holdings to the eastern front; and after the war the autographs could not be found. It was only in the late 1970s that they were rediscovered, in Poland; now they are housed at the Jagiellońska Library in Kraków. More recently, scholars have also identified several manuscript parts copies owned and used by Mozart and his family to perform the works, both in Salzburg and in Vienna. In keeping with the spirit of Hutchings's original listing, an update on the locations of these sources is given here:

K.37, 39–41   Autographs at the Jagiellońska Library, Kraków
K.175   Autograph lost; copy used by the Mozart family in Salzburg, Archabbey of St Peter's, Salzburg

K.238   Autograph at the Library of Congress, Washington, DC; performing copy used by the Mozart family in Salzburg at the Archabbey of St Peter's, Salzburg

K.242   Autograph at the Jagiellońska Library, Kraków; copy possibly used by Mozart to perform the work in Vienna at the Staatsbibliothek zu Berlin (Berlin). Another copy, possibly with Mozart's autograph corrections in the parts, and used by him in Mannheim and Paris in 1777 and 1778, at the Stanford University Library, Stanford, California

K.246   Autograph at the Jagiellońska Library, Kraków; copy used by the Mozart family in Salzburg at the Archabbey of St Peter's, Salzburg

K.271   Autograph at the Jagiellońska Library, Kraków; copy used by the Mozart family in Salzburg at the Archabbey of St Peter's, Salzburg

K.365   Autograph at the Jagiellońska Library, Kraków; copy used by the Mozart family in Salzburg at the Archabbey of St Peter's, Salzburg; copy used by Mozart to perform the concerto in Vienna at the Státní Zámek a Zahrady, Kroměříž, Czech Republic

K.413   Autograph at the Jagiellońska Library, Kraków; copy, now incomplete, brought by Mozart to Salzburg in 1783 at the Archabbey of St Peter's, Salzburg

K.414   Autograph at the Jagiellońska Library, Kraków; copy, now incomplete, brought by Mozart to Salzburg in 1783 at the Archabbey of St Peter's, Salzburg

K.415   Autograph at the Jagiellońska Library, Kraków; brought by Mozart to Salzburg in 1783 at the Archabbey of St Peter's, Salzburg

K.449   Autograph at the Jagiellońska Library, Kraków; copy used by the Mozart family in Salzburg at the Archabbey of St Peter's, Salzburg

K.450   Autograph at the Thüringische Landesbibliothek, Weimar

K.451   Autograph at the Jagiëllońska Library, Kraków; copy used by the Mozart family in Salzburg at the Archabbey of St Peter's, Salzburg

K.453   Autograph at the Jagiellońska Library, Kraków

K.456   Autograph at the Jagiellońska Library, Kraków

K.459   Autograph at the Jagiellońska Library, Kraków

K.466   Autograph at the Bibliothek und Archiv, Gesellschaft der Musikfreunde, Vienna; copy used by the Mozart family in Salzburg at the Archabbey of St Peter's Salzburg

viii FOREWORD

K.467 Autograph at the Pierpont Morgan Library, New York
K.482 Autograph at the Jagiellońska Library, Kraków
K.488 Autograph at the Bibliothèque Nationale, Paris
K.491 Autograph at the British Library, London
K.503 Autograph at the Jagiellońska Library, Kraków
K.537 Autograph at the Library of Congress, Washington, DC
K.595 Autograph at the Jagiellońska Library, Kraków

London
October 1997

CONTENTS

NOTE

Books showing the structure and content of a series of works rarely engage readers who are not already lovers of at least some of the music dealt with, and it seems plain that when, in the late 'thirties, I embarked on this study, a revival of interest in the concertos was 'in the air'; it is good to note that orchestras and pianists are playing some of Mozart's concertos better and more frequently. Some of the finest are still infrequently played, but others have secured multiple recordings, and all of them are available as Vol. 2 of Philips's Complete Edition. In the concert hall, as on some recordings we still have to endure lengthy, complex, and inept cadenzas which seems inexcusable in those concertos for which we have Mozart's own candenzas.

A.H., 1979

ACKNOWLEDGEMENTS

I wish to thank Prof. C. M. Girdlestone, author of *Mozart et ses concertos pour piano*, for generously putting at my disposal the information and opinions he had sifted in preparing his study, and for lending me editions of works by pre-Mozartian concertists. I also wish to thank Mr. Hyatt King, of the British Museum, for similar help. Acknowledgement is also due to Miss Emily Anderson and Messrs. Macmillan & Co. Ltd., for permitting me to quote pertinent extracts from Mozart's letters from the three-volume edition of *The Letters of Mozart and his Family*, translated and edited by Miss Anderson.

THE MOZART AUTOGRAPHS

IN 1869 the Prussian State Library in Berlin acquired the Mozartian collection of Otto Jahn (1813–69), philologist and archaeologist, whose four-volume biography, *W. A. Mozart*, containing interesting portraits and facsimiles, had been published in 1867. Jahn's death terminated similar work which he was preparing in respect of Beethoven and other composers. In 1873 the same library acquired the largest of all collections of autographs, formerly the property of Johann Anton André (1775–1842), the publisher who in 1799 had bought from Mozart's widow all the composer's music then in her possession.

Therefore the bulk of concerto autographs is to be found in the Berlin Library, though a few of the pieces once owned by André are privately owned still. The following table gives the present home of all concerto autographs not acquired by the Prussian State Library.

Concerto in D major, K.175. Berlin, F. A. Grassnick.
Concerto in B flat, K.238. Vienna, Wittgenstein family.
Concerto in B flat, K.450. Weimar, Grand Ducal Library.
Concerto in D minor, K.466. Vienna, Gesellschaft der Musikfreunde.
Concerto in C major, K.467. Vienna, Wittgenstein family.
Concerto in A major, K.488. Paris, Conservatoire de Musique.
Concerto in C minor, K.491. London, Royal College of Music.
Concerto in D major, K.537. Ixelles (Brussels), D. N. Heinemann.

This shows that Berlin holds the autographs of sixteen original keyboard concertos by Mozart, and those of the four early pieces (K.37, 39, 40, 41) arranged by him in concerto form. Thanks to the photostat copies made by A. von Hoboken, scholars may inspect facsimiles of K.466 and K.467 at the Vienna National Library, and one may hope that very soon photostats of these and other manuscripts which are privately owned will be included in British libraries.

THEMATIC GUIDE TO
THE CLAVIER CONCERTOS OF
WOLFGANG AMADEUS MOZART
1756–91

TOGETHER WITH DATES OF COMPOSITION

1. EARLY ARRANGEMENTS FROM SONATAS BY OTHER COMPOSERS

K.37.

1767.

K.39.

1767.

K.40.

1767.

K.41.

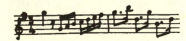

1767.

2. THE SALZBURG CONCERTOS

K.175

Dec. 1773.

K.238.

Jan. 1776.

K.242.

Feb. 1776.

(For 3 claviers)

K.246.

Apr. 1776.

K.271.

Jan. 1777.

K.365.

1779–80, exact date unknown.

(For 2 claviers)

3. THE VIENNA CONCERTOS

A. *The 1782 works*

K.382.

Mar. 1782.

(New rondo for K.175)

K.413.

Autumn 1782.

K.414.

Autumn 1782.

K.415.

Autumn 1782.

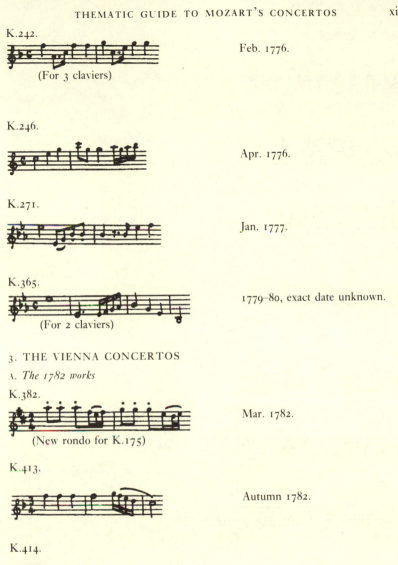

B. *The mature series*

K.449.

Feb. 1784.

K.450.

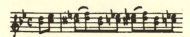

Mar. 1784.

K.451.

Mar. 1784.

K.453.

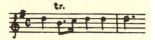

Apr. 1784.

K.456.

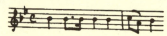

Sept. 1784.

K.459.

Dec. 1784.

K.466.

Feb. 1785.

K.467.

Mar. 1785.

K.482.

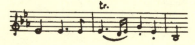

Dec. 1785.

K.488.

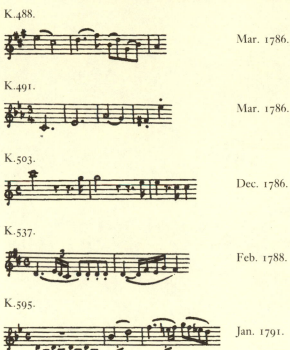

Mar. 1786.

K.491.

Mar. 1786.

K.503.

Dec. 1786.

K.537.

Feb. 1788.

K.595.

Jan. 1791.

The revised Eulenberg pocket edition, prepared by Dr. F. Blume after examination of original manuscripts or the Hoboken photostat copies at Vienna, is recommended to students in respect of any concertos for which it is available. It is a pity that, 'for technical reasons', Blume was unable to indicate the continuo functions of the piano in non-solo passages. In this detail alone the student or performer must prepare his own score, so to speak. Places in which he would write *tasto solo* are not easy to decide in later concertos, though places wherein silence is required from the piano are fairly obvious, e.g. those consisting of dialogue between wind instruments and soloist. The performer's guide in this matter is the sounding or silence of the string bass.

Though Breitkopf and Härtel issued seventeen volumes of Mozart's works 1798–1816, the first edition of the piano concertos in score (from K.238 onwards) was published by Richault of Paris *c.* 1850. Destruction of Breitkopf and Härtel's premises during the war made a new Collected Edition necessary.

CHAPTER I

INTRODUCTION. MOZART AND THE CONCERTO

HAVING discovered the spellings 'Mozerth' and 'Mozer' in parish registers around Salzburg, anti-Semitic authorities order the destruction of all Mozart's work except a few representative scores to be deposited in the Museum of Degenerate Art. What shall we spare? Of course the operas, and then—the symphonies or the concertos? If Worcester or St. Paul's must be destroyed, for which shall we plead? We may like gothic and dislike Wren, whose dome is a funnel, whose ornament domestic; St. Paul's may be an amazing hybrid, but we shall spare the only St. Paul's and we shall retain the Mozart concertos. They, too, are amazing hybrids and their artist something of an engineer. Mozart alone enriched with a large number of vital examples the most highly organized of all purely instrumental forms; for the clavier concerto is a complicated blend of solo sonata, concerto grosso, and ritornellic aria. Twenty-three times he regimented the welter of material which makes a concerto of the Mozartian order, and at least sixteen times he thereby created a work of masterly beauty. Other composers wrote symphonies and quartets of high quality in greater number than did Mozart, though many declare that not one of them is equal to the very best Mozart symphony or quartet; in the realm of concerto, however, opinion need not be controversial, since it is concerned with quantity and not quality.

This study is based on the conviction that Mozart, and Mozart alone, perceived the principles by which the slender entertainment of Schobert, Christian Bach, Vanhall, and Wagenseil, could be transformed into an art form which should in no way develop along the same lines as symphony and sonata. Later were to come many beautiful works called concertos, but all except those of Brahms are far more simple in structure, since they revert to the two-subject hybridization of sonata form from which Mozart's concerto began. At his maturity as a concertist, Mozart required at least four important subjects, some not heard from soloist, some not played by the orchestra.

Mozart's concertos may be misconceived and badly performed if people suppose the later art form to have sprung from his models by a process of natural selection. It did not. But for Mozart, the later form would have shown itself to be what it is when not infused with genius—successor to the simple *concerto galant*. Those concertos of Beethoven's five which are worthy to stand beside the best of Mozart's twenty-three owe their greatness to Beethoven's greatness, no small part of which lay in his deliberate adoption of Mozartian ideals. As a result of post-Beethovenian reversion to sonata type, very few composers grappled successfully with concerto. If solo and orchestra use the same subject matter without wearisome repetition, either the orchestra becomes mere accompanist or framework to a brilliant sonata, or else a grand and fearsome piano part must vary the themes of a basically simple form.

The piano concerto seems to be 'played out'. The nineteenth century, hey-day of fine pianism, pushed its own type of virtuosity to a logical limit, and when sonata-concerto has been used for the last time without conscious archaism, composers will recognize that lessons may be taken from the structure and technique which Beethoven did not despise.

Mozart explained no structural principles in writing; nor did he emulate Gluck in prefaces and manifestoes to operas. One or two precious letters show that he was conscious of every dramatic detail of his stage works. He tells his father, for instance, that the oracle in *Idomeneo* must not have too long a recitative, for the ghost in *Hamlet* would be more awe-inspiring if it had less to say; and though we have still less from his pen concerning concerto problems, his consistent application to them is evident in the works which so gloriously surmounted them. Before the series of master-works inaugurated by the Concerto in E flat, K. 449, each specimen advances from its predecessor in number of themes and in organization.

Just as *Figaro* revitalized opera buffa while retaining (indeed embracing) its characteristics and limitations, so the Mozartian concerto retained the spirit of a fashionable, entertaining, and money-making piece. 'Here', says Eric Blom, 'we enter a world of enchanted artificiality', and one can have little patience with those who deny this plain fact, or who consider the best concertos to be the most symphonic and Beethovenian.

Rarely has any composer received the rapid access of adulation that has been poured upon Mozart during the past few decades, as a reaction to former dullness of perception. Only publishers and Salzburg caterers can have vested interests in the raising of his stock, and if sheer musical snobbery or a mass epidemic of the thurifer mentality can cause a literary stampede, why have there been no parallel movements in the cult of other composers? This study adds nothing to the pile of devotional literature. Mozart was late in reaching sexual puberty, and, though in artists mental puberty often comes first, the same weaknesses which kept Mozart to his parents' apron-strings, and to a religious orthodoxy not based upon deep thinking, also made him imitative and conservative in matters musical until, without proclamation, he dared what no previous musician had dared —to strike out on his own, independent of patron, relatives, or fixed sources of income. Before he did so, his music departed from pre-cedent in only two manifestations, opera and concerto. The least valuable Salzburg concerto is more interesting than any by older or contemporary concertists, and one of them, the first of the E flat Concertos, K. 271, is nothing short of revolutionary. It proclaimed once and for ever that a concerto should be organically unlike sym-phony or sonata.

Since instrumental music can have no permanent value unless it expresses, not just apes, human emotions, what of the spiritual con-tent of the earlier concertos? Some of the Salzburg works reveal that emotional growth which preceded the composer's full physical development. Others seem to contain little more than the pseudo-emotion which Mozart's age called 'sentiment', and which is endear-ing to period-fanciers and Mozart-adorers. Mozart found his greatest, most sincere range of expression in opera, and the most beautiful passages in the concertos are those wherein operatic Mozart quivers beneath the *galanterie* and virtuosity of the concert room. Operatic Mozart first came to glorious maturity in *Idomeneo* and *Die Entführung* (1781 and 1782 respectively). Just before the production of the second of the operas mentioned, Mozart began to write those con-certos which are the finest of their kind.

CHAPTER II

THE MOZARTIAN CONCEPTION

(1) *First Movements*

IN 1903 Tovey wrote his monograph *The Classical Concerto*,[1] and showed what the word 'concerto' meant to those who first dignified it. Had either theorists or performers mended their ways, there would be no need to write an essay which adds nothing to Tovey's; but since untruth is repeated in text-books, and people applaud the artistic untruth of vulgarity, it is still a duty to spell out Tovey slowly. They are neither bad text-books nor bad performers who travesty Mozart's conception of concerto; they have not recognized the generating principles of the most complex instrumental form yet known in western music. Mozartian concerto is a Mistress Quickly—'she's neither fish nor flesh, and a man knows not where to have her'; among the pile of books about Mozart few explain the form which, after opera, held his interest most consistently, and the only study of the complete concertos in any language is C. M. Girdlestone's fascinating *Mozart et ses concertos pour piano*, published as late as 1939.

There is no such work as a 'typical Mozart concerto', but the Concerto in D minor, K. 466, is one of the best known and most representative specimens of his mature work as a concertist. By analysing this work we shall find how vastly different were his purposes in a concerto from his purposes in sonata or symphony. Let us therefore begin examination of its first movement, and see the principles by which it was composed, stating what we find in the simplest language. Without the cadenza, the movement is 398 bars long; it has six *clearly marked* sections, in three of which the piano is silent.

1. Orchestral prelude	76 bars.	
2. Piano with orchestra	94 „	
3. Orchestra alone	22 „	
4. Piano with orchestra	63 „	
5. Piano with orchestra	110 „	
6. Orchestra alone	33 „	interrupted by cadenza.

[1] Reprinted at the beginning of *Essays in Musical Analysis*, vol. iii (Oxford University Press).

1. Theme 'A'

2. Theme 'B'

3. Theme 'E'

4. Theme 'X'

5. Theme 'Y'

6. Theme 'C'

7. Theme 'C'

Thus, the only demarcation which is not made by complete change of performer is that between sections 4 and 5; it is clearly made by the music, however, since section 5 begins like the opening of the concerto, *for which reason alone it is called a recapitulation.* Every Mozart and Beethoven concerto shows these six sections.

We now look at section 1, the orchestral prelude, whose five musical paragraphs are easily separated by Mozart's five expression marks *p, f, p, f, p,* and we label them A, B, C, D, E. The whole prelude ends, as it began, in D minor. The solo then enters, and we note four conditions of its entry:

1. It enters *alone* (Ex. 4).
2. The tune it plays *has not been heard previously.*
3. Since no tune in the prelude is to be used more often in the course of the concerto, this first solo tune must be *important.*
4. It is essentially *a tune for a keyboard instrument. No other instrument than the piano plays this tune during the piece.* Its octave leap and drop of a sixth sound clear on a piano, but would be ungrateful and ineffective on violins, unless they altered the tune's character by such devices as vibrato, portamento, or nuance.

After twelve solo bars, the piano plays what cannot be called melody but brilliant figuration, or *bravura*; the orchestra joins quietly to support the *bravura* work; then the solo is silent while the orchestra plays theme A (Ex. 1) with which it previously opened the prelude. It has not gone far with this return or ritornello of A, before the solo returns a compliment; true, it cannot support the orchestra, but it can add to its texture and give rhythmic punch to the bass. We have examined enough to note that, in Mozartian concerto, *the partners share thematic matter equally.* It may be pointed out that the solo has opportunity for display, with mere support from the orchestra, for a lengthy passage at the end of this section, ending with a cadential shake in F, the relative major key. (In major-key concertos, the second section ends with a shake in the dominant cadence.) Yet this *bravura* does not make the solo the more important of the partners, for the orchestra has three of the six sections all to itself, and the passages in which the solo can speak entirely alone are few and short.

As if to emphasize the equal footing of the partners, the next *new* tune requires the contribution of both (Ex. 5). This is the last of the tunes to appear for the first time, and we can now arrange them all

in a diagram, wherein orchestral tunes have capital letters, made
into corresponding small letters when translated into piano idiom
—see Exx. 6 and 7. Section 2 now receives a title which is self-explanatory.[1]

1. Orchestral prelude	A	B	C	D	E.
2. Solo exposition	x	A	Bb	y	c Bravura.
3. Orchestra alone	B	E.			
4. Middle section	xA	xA	xA	A.	
5. Recapitulation	Aa	Bb	y	c	Bravura.
6. Orchestra alone	B	C	D	E.	

(The diagram does not make allowance for a cadenza.)

Next we have to find a functional label for the two sections still
simply called 'orchestra alone'. They use only themes which come
in the prelude, and we are therefore justified in calling sections 3
and 6 'First Ritornello' and 'Final Ritornello' respectively. Like
the prelude to a Handel aria, they return when the soloist takes rest,
and round off or frame the solo sections; they do so in single themes
during concertante sections, but sections 3 and 6 are entirely ritornellic and of considerable length. *The principle of ritornello* is
therefore of great importance in the Mozartian conception of
concerto.

But to organize ritornelli with concertante material in such a way
as to impart the astounding variety which we recognize at a glance
from the diagram, Mozart uses also what I propose to call *the principle
of open ends*, or more simply, *the principle of jig-saw*. In the prelude
we see that theme B leads into theme C, but later on we have Bb–y,
B–E, and in the last *full* ritornello B–C once more! Thus B is like
one of the pieces in a jig-saw puzzle which is capable of fitting into
any one of three other jigs; and if one end of B fits the other end of
three different themes, then at least two of those themes have an open
'other end'.

If ever we are deluded into supposing that the only function of
the long orchestral prelude is to give the main solo themes a sort of
preliminary canter, the diagram of any single first movement will
correct us. The prelude may be debased into that simple affair by
later composers, though most of them have the sense to truncate the
prelude to a mere introduction. True, Mozart writes one important
theme, not always the first, upon which expository argument is based,

[1] I have retained traditional section labels though I think those used by Denis
Forman (*Mozart's Concerto Form*, Cassell 1970) to be better than mine.

and which the solo repeats or translates into keyboard idiom; but the most important function of Mozart's prelude is to make us familiar with materials to be used in ritornelli, whether singly in concertante sections, or in variously condensed and associated groups at the two big orchestral ritornelli. What a scheme is implicit in the Mozartian concerto prelude! In comparison with the wealth and intricacy of a Mozartian first movement, how simple and dull an affair is a scheme like the following:

Prelude	A	B.	
Exposition	A	B	Bravura.
Ritornello	A.		
Development	A or B.		
Recapitulation	A	B.	
Ritornello	A	Cadenza A.	

Needless to say, the most notorious keyboard mountebanks have rarely put forward so absurd a 'structure'; the nineteenth-century virtuosi gave us either an amorphous affair in which prelude remained while ritornelli were mixed with a welter of pianism, or else a sort of piano sonata with accompaniment, in which an occasional theme is played by the orchestra. In this type of composition, prelude and ritornelli are mere frames, cut down to a minimum and sometimes disappearing completely. Many a fine work was written in this 'framed sonata' form. Schumann actually called his biggest sonata 'concerto without orchestra'. These remarks intend no disparagement to the concertos of Chopin, Schumann, Grieg, or even Rachmaninoff; but it seems important to point out that the word 'concerto' has come to denote two entirely different types of composition, the later a much more simple affair than the earlier. (So simple, indeed, that unless we are held by brilliant variation of themes, or by fine pianism, we take little interest in the structure of virtuoso concertos after the point of recapitulation is past.)

But our diagram has even yet done less than justice to the Mozartian conception of first movement; it shows the ritornello principle and the jig-saw principle, but it suggests that Mozart *manipulates* a mass of short themes, and that those who came after him thought in bigger dimensions. If we look once more at the prelude, we shall see, however, that our algebra has been somewhat too finicky, and that the following diagram, drawn to scale, gives a better idea of Mozart's outlay. Orchestral sections are enclosed in thick lines and free passages are shaded.

Concerto in D minor, K. 466

Prelude	A --- a | B --- b | C	76 bars.
Exposition	X ------ AB | Y ------ b	94 ,,
First full ritornello	A --- a | C	22 ,,
Middle section	XA XA XA	63 ,,
Recapitulation	A --- a | Y --- b	110 ,,
Final ritornello	B cadenza b | C	33 ,,

Now let us turn to the account of Mozart's concertos in English standard books which deal with musical form. We see the use to which X is put as the perfect antithesis and complement to the orchestra's A; this is particularly emphasized in the middle section. Yet the *Oxford History of Music*, which gives unduly scant space to the concerto before Beethoven, regards this X, and its brothers in other concertos, as an extra and introductory theme to the exposition proper. How can we regard X and Y as any less essential to Mozart's scheme than are A and B?

In his *Form in Music*,[1] Stewart Macpherson allows only the following words upon the Mozartian concerto:

'It was not until the time of Mozart that the concerto definitely assumed the form with which we are now familiar, viz. that of a work, usually of the dimensions of a sonata, for a solo instrument with orchestral accompaniment. The concertos of Mozart and his immediate successors are mostly on the three-movement plan, and consist of an Allegro in sonata form, with a notable modification—the *Double Exposition*, the plan of which will be discerned by the following diagram:

Exposition I. (Orchestra.)	*Exposition II.* (Solo with accompaniment.)
1st subject in Tonic.	1st subject in Tonic.
2nd subject in Tonic.	2nd subject in Dominant or Relative Major, both subjects being presented with a good deal of florid ornamentation for the soloist.

'The development and recapitulation usually open with orchestral tuttis of some importance. . . .'

Macpherson then analyses not a Mozart concerto but the single

[1] Joseph Williams.

classical concerto that fits the preconceived scheme—Beethoven's
C minor, which Tovey shows to be Beethoven's one mistake. (The
mistake in structural procedure was immediately corrected by Beethoven, and Tovey's demonstration of the fact does not make the
C minor any less fine a work.) Every single statement made in
Macpherson's description, except that giving the number of movements, is as untrue for Mozart as it is true for the nineteenth-century
concertists, and a few rhetorical questions, though seeming to be ill-
natured, will help us to recognize the difference between the two
conceptions. There are as many variants to my D minor diagram as
there are Mozart concertos, yet not one, not even the exceptional
K. 488 (q.v.) tallies with Macpherson's scheme. If any of the following questions is unanswerable, something of Mozart's purpose
will be revealed by admitting the fact:

1. If K. 466 has a double exposition, which are the principal subjects, A or x, B or y? (See Exx. 1, 2, 4, and 5.)
2. If both subjects are presented 'with a good deal of free matter',
where is it? There are twelve bars *bravura* at the end of the
exposition and fifteen at the end of the recapitulation—in a
movement of nearly 400 bars.
3. Does the recapitulation merely repeat the order of themes in the
exposition?
4. If 'tuttis of some importance' *open* each concertante section,

   (*a*) Why do they use only materials from the prelude?
   (*b*) Why do they burst in *forte*, not with the quiet, shudder-
   ing A?
   (*c*) Why do they always follow the long cadential shake which
   is used *only at the conclusion* of a solo or concertante
   section?

If final proof were needed of the propriety of the label 'ritornello' in
preference to 'opening tutti', we have it from Mozart. The orchestral
sections, and they alone, are given an unmistakable sense of finality
by being rounded off with an exquisite theme (C in our final diagram);
its haunting F major version at the end of the first ritornello is quoted
in Ex. 3 (E in previous diagram).

The organization implicit in one of Mozart's concerto preludes
can well be tested by following the fortunes of a single theme. We
have already noticed the open ends of B, but a theme may not be
merely ritornellic. Consider theme A in its various positions:

1. It opens the concerto and sets a stormy atmosphere.
2. It returns as a single ritornello-theme after the solo's x, showing itself utterly in contrast to the keyboard theme—this is an important juxtaposition.
3. It leads the first full ritornello, which is highly condensed.
4. It generates the development section by its repeated opposition to x.
5. It marks the recapitulation.
6. It is purposely missing in the final ritornello, which begins with B.

It should be noted that no two sections follow the same order of material, and that if Mozart has given prominence to any single theme in one section he contrives to omit it in the next. The theme which sheds its stormy personality most powerfully over the whole movement, and which is the one uppermost in our minds as we come away from a performance, is C in the first diagram, B in the second; it occurs three times on the orchestra and three times in a keyboard translation (Exx. 6 and 7).

Some of Mozart's later concertos, e.g. K. 503 and K. 595, combine the lavish organization of themes with a paradoxical economy and breadth; they approach Beethoven's intensity of purpose while retaining an idiom as Mozartian as ever. It is often observed that Beethoven improved the sonata forms by his unwillingness tamely to repeat his expositions in his recapitulations, and by his generation of intense movement in middle sections. Mozart's age and conservatism felt no need for these improvements in sonata and symphony, but Mozart must have been aware of the dullness of a repetitive concerto, wherein prelude, exposition, and recapitulation served the same dishes in the same order. Let it be remembered that Beethoven wrote five piano concertos to Mozart's twenty-three, and only two of them excel, as Beethoven, against many which excel as Mozart. In the domain of symphony the order of merit is reversed. We are considering only the *number* of great concertos and great symphonies, since few occupations could be more unprofitable than the setting of these two giants as rivals in quality. We know that Beethoven admired and played the Mozart concertos, and that his finest works in the form flatter the Mozartian conception. The difference between them as concertists is seen very clearly in their different methods of writing the recapitulatory section; Beethoven's artistry works *on* a few big materials and presents them with new treatment; Mozart's works *with* a mass of smaller materials, reshuffling and condensing them. Only after a struggle for which his life was too short could Beethoven have brought the number of his great concertos up to that of his symphonies and quartets. With Mozart's particular type of artistry the case is reversed; there are not so much as half the number of first-rate symphonies as there are first-rate concertos from Mozart's pen.

Acquaintance with the later, more simple form known as concerto makes us listen to Beethoven's concertos with prejudiced ears; the interplay of solo and orchestra, despite some new master-strokes, is less subtle and less ubiquitous than in Mozart; the pianist has to be both lighter and heavier, and his brilliant passages need more than musicianship and good training as a player. They demand a certain type of player, whereas Mozart's figurations are effective from a dozen players all of different type, if they play accurately, with control and with a first-rate technique. One feature distinguishes a Beethoven concerto from a Mozart concerto, and that feature is not any one of Beethoven's so-called innovations; Mozart made a far greater number of innovations to the concerto than Beethoven did. Indeed Mozart's experiments with concerto are to be paralleled only by Beethoven's with the symphony and sonata forms. Did Beethoven astound folk when the solo was heard in the opening bars of his fourth and fifth concertos? Mozart had used the gambit as early as his Salzburg days, in the E flat Concerto, K. 271, and he had more taste than to repeat the method. Did Beethoven appear unconventional by opening the first symphony in sub-dominant, instead of tonic harmony? Mozart did the same thing, with less advertisement, in the A major Concerto, K. 488. The one feature which gloriously distinguishes a Beethoven from a Mozart concerto is the presence of Beethoven, and that presence makes itself felt technically by the tenacity of purpose evident in a few pregnant themes, consistently developed and pervading the whole movement. Beethoven's 'middle section' is always a development section: sometimes Mozart's is nothing of the sort, as the reader may observe by attempting to draw a diagram of K. 450. Sometimes, though Mozart may develop a certain theme to the exclusion of other material in his middle sections, the theme chosen is a subsidiary one, or a little 'extra' tailpiece from the ritornello, like the 'Come to the cookhouse door' tune in K. 456, of which the plan is as follows:

Concerto in B flat, K. 456

Prelude	A	B	C	D	E	F.
Exposition	A	B	x	D	E	y.
First ritornello	B	F.				
Middle section	z	F	F	F	Free.	

It will be noticed that in this concerto, A, a small but effective opening gesture, does not open either ritornelli or middle section; by definition it is bound to open the recapitulation, or we should not recognize the recapitulation as such. Mozart is too sensitive to exalt so small a thing to first place in any other section, so he devises a delicious pianistic flight, z, to open his middle section, and z is not heard anywhere else in the movement (see Ex. 100).

Middle sections, as much as all other sections which follow the solo exposition, are guided by the same wise economy which sought to give open ends to one or two of the themes in the prelude; for a third principle in the Mozartian concerto conception is but the same which caused the jig-saw technique. Let us call it *the principle of variety in the order of themes*. Though Mozart's finest structures are those of his last concertos, which make the middle section a real development, the principle just named may prevent the adoption of formal, imitative, or metabolic development. An examination of the last concerto, whose themes are entirely Mozartian and not even remotely Beethovenian, shows a most marked tendency towards economy and breadth, while the previous great concerto (the immediate predecessor in D major is not a concerto to be reckoned in the great series; I am thinking here of the C major, K. 503) actually shows a motif, of three repeating quavers, which is common to three of the five main themes of prelude and exposition. From this we must not infer that Mozart would ever have written themes like Beethoven, or have used so few as did the later master; we can see the falsity of such an inference by noticing just one section of a late Mozart concerto, the section which might be supposed most Beethovenian, namely the middle section which in late concertos is rightly called a development. It will be seen that Mozart deals with a whole theme —perhaps of four bars' length—as he modulates, even though he has to repeat it six times. There is no dullness in his procedure, especially when it involves the astounding counterpoint of K. 503 (see Ex. 167); but such development is more lyrical, more leisurely, more obviously 'middle sectional' than are the short-rhythm, kinetic developments of Beethoven which, instead of spreading themselves before us, recognize no static beauty apart from their intense purpose—to exploit the possibilities of the main subjects (as in the climax of a play) and to point to the apotheosis of those subjects in the recapitulation. In a Beethoven concerto the cadenza marks a point of climax, as does the dramatic reprise after the middle section; in Mozart the cadenza and the point of reprise are usually paralleled in beauty and interest by a dozen other points.

'Mozart's opening tuttis are among the highest triumphs of their art in their command of expectant exposition', says Tovey, and we have seen that the tutti is only partly expository—in the D minor Concerto it is expository only for the orchestra. By definition, the prelude cannot itself be a ritornello, but it makes the pleasure of small and large ritornelli available throughout the movement. If the prelude and the organization which it implies are not the very basis of Mozartian concerto, let us imagine a prelude which is less highly organized. There is no need to imagine; we can find it in concertos before Mozart as much as in concertos after him. The two Haydn clavier concertos still available in modern editions, those in D and G, are made of pleasant materials which grow a little wearisome, since the Mozartian construction is impossible. Haydn's concertos are simple and entertaining, but not great. Now since Haydn wrote a greater number of first-rate symphonies than did Mozart, we must acknowledge that it was the latter's recognition of the difference in conception between ideal concerto and ideal symphony that made him incomparably the greatest of classical concertists. To think of the eighteenth-century concerto is to think primarily of Mozart, and we must either be fools enough to regard every later concerto as a decadent work or else we must judge the nineteenth-century concerto by non-Mozartian criteria.

Did Mozart leave nothing to the inspiration of the moment? Was nothing written 'at the instrument'—for Mozart was not one of those liars who deny the presence of a keyboard in their workshops—was he a spawning automaton? We are surely safe in supposing that, either at the nefarious keyboard, or while folding his napkin, Mozart exercised his artistry in deciding which of his materials should be elided, extended, or advanced. One curious effect of Mozart's freedom, in a form which would limit another man, is that we come away from a performance of one of his concertos humming not always the main theme but a transition tune, common to band and solo. If Mozart's concertos are machine-made, so are Bach's 'Forty-eight'. At any point in the texture of Bach or of Mozart, melody will sprout not only in so-called free writing (of which there is little, and that little in specified places), but in the main concertante sections, exposition, middle section, and recapitulation. Those who would like to test this statement may try to draw a diagram of K. 482 in E flat, or even of the early K. 271 in the same key; they will find the resultant algebra very difficult to bring to its lowest terms, for tunes grow into other tunes.

A short and simple definition of a Mozartian concerto-movement cannot be given, for it is not a short and simple affair. In all music there is but one more complicated form than concerto, namely the operatic act with five or six characters, each preserving personality while contributing to the ensemble and passing through various moods and situations. It is therefore not by any means a coincidence that the same mind excelled in the development of these two complicated forms and guided the first of them through the most dangerous period of its history. When Mozart first approached it, the concerto was a slight and fashionable form of entertainment; so was opera buffa. Despite exceptional works like the C minor Concerto and *Don Giovanni*, he kept both forms entertaining and fashionable, seeming to glory in the fact that they were entertaining while raising them to the highest artistic level.

To summarize; the organization of first movements in Mozartian piano concertos is based upon:

1. The principle of ritornello, with ritornellic materials given in the orchestral prelude.
2. The principle of jig-saw, or themes with open ends.
3. The principle of varied order when themes are heard more than once.
4. The principle of equality of status between orchestra and soloist.

(2) *Slow Movements*

One measure of the greatness of Mozart's slow movements in his piano concertos is the large variety of their forms and conceptions; whether we like or dislike any particular Andante, we can be sure that Mozart's choice was entirely his own, unless he was writing the movement against time for a certain occasion. Now there is hardly one poor first movement in all twenty-three concertos, yet 'the interest retires' a little in one or two concertos (only one or two) after the first movement has been performed. This opinion is a personal one; it so happens that I feel this true of the slow movement to the D minor Concerto. For me, it is repetitive, languorous, and unduly simple, even without the vulgar 'interpretation' which I have rarely failed to hear from a soloist. Another listener may be enraptured by that movement, and my failure to share his rapture may be due to my own dullness. The point I wish to bring out by this mention of people's likes and dislikes is that, although different folk have expressed their dissatisfaction with this or that andante or finale, everybody who likes Mozart is satisfied that, on the whole, the greatest of him is found in first movements, or in variation forms, or in finales (such as those to K. 449 in E flat, K. 459 in F, or this D minor work) which are structurally more severe than text-book rondo. Yet we have seen that Mozart was free, in his slow movements, to let form and inspiration go hand in hand. It is obvious, therefore, that Mozart's work was usually best when mental effort was needed. What great yet simple songs did he write, except those created under the pressure of an operatic situation? Is not many a minuet uninspired? Has any musician deeply enjoyed the whole of the Haffner Serenade?

Of several forms of slow movement found in Mozart's concertos, two are *not* built in simple integral strophes (as is the Romanza of the D minor Concerto), but demand musical thinking in long periods. These are (1) the binary sonata-form and (2) the extended aria-form. The second of them employs the ritornello principle, though on a smaller scale than in first movements. It is precisely these more complicated types, together with the variations used in the slow movements of K. 450, K. 456, and K. 482, which Mozart makes the vehicles of his most inspired andantes, and it is hard to explain why he showed as great an affection for the simple strophic romanza as he did for a glorious integral conception like the sonata-adagio in F sharp minor within the A major Concerto, K. 488, or for the superb and poignant aria-andante within the G major Concerto, K. 453. It is no less hard to understand how musicians can compare the worth of a simple strophic movement with the deeply poetic G minor Variations of K. 456.

Some writers have noted that the romanza became increasingly a favourite with Mozart in his last years, but the point can be exaggerated. Many an early slow movement was in simple strophic form before the composer had begun to use the actual term 'romanza'. His first use of that title is in the Serenade for Wind Instruments in B flat, K. 361, written in 1780, that is to say, after his break with the Archbishop. For what it is worth, I submit a list of the concertos, with the type of slow movement used in each:

Salzburg:
    K. 175 in D. Andante in G. Sonata (R).
    K. 238 in B flat. Andante in E flat. Aria-sonata.
    K. 242 in F (3 claviers). Adagio in B flat. Sonata with development.
    K. 246 in C. Andante in F. Aria.
    K. 271 in E flat. Andantino in C minor. Aria.
    K. 365 in E flat (2 claviers). Andante in B flat. Binary dialogue with coda.

1782 set:

K. 413 in F. Larghetto in B flat. Binary aria, strophic.
K. 414 in A. Andante in D. Binary aria, strophic.
K. 415 in C. Andante in F. Ternary with coda.

Vienna concertos:

K. 449 in E flat. Andantino in B flat. Irregular ternary with coda.
K. 450 in B flat. Andante in B flat. Variations with coda.
K. 451 in D. Andante in G. Shorter rondo (R).
K. 453 in G. Andante in C. Aria, strophic.
K. 456 in B flat. Andante in G minor. Variations.
K. 459 in F. Allegretto in C. Pastoral. Sonata.
K. 466 in D minor. Romanza in B flat. Romanza, strophic.
K. 467 in C. Andante in F. Irregular non-strophic (R).
K. 482 in E flat. Andante in C minor. Interrupted variations.
K. 488 in A. Adagio in F sharp minor.[1] Sonata with coda.
K. 491 in C minor. Larghetto in E flat. Romanza.
K. 503 in C. Andante in F. Sonata without development.
K. 537 in D. Larghetto in A. Romanza.
K. 595 in B flat. Larghetto in E flat. Romanza.

The sign 'R' put after a title means 'Reverie', and owes its presence to my reading of Girdlestone's *Mozart et ses concertos pour piano*.

Recognizing the difficulty of any attempt to classify them according to their forms, Girdlestone shows the *spiritual* affinities which link together a chain of slow movements from Salzburg days to the time of the last Vienna concertos. Movements which are spirtually akin may not be alike formally; with Mozart, choice of key had powerful spiritual significance, as we see in the C minor andantes to concertos in E flat. By examining the content rather than classifying the form of Mozart's andantes, Girdlestone gives us more insight into the composer's mind, and in doing so separates, purely for convenience, the moods portrayed in the *andante galant*, the meditative andante, the andante cantabile or romanza, the elegiac andante, the dramatic andante, and the andante-reverie or 'dream andante'.

Those who possess records of the third of Mozart's four concertos in C, K. 467, must have been surprised and enchanted at their first hearing of a 'dream andante', for perusal of the score reveals little of the actual effect, even with the most imaginative and experienced score-taster, and there is little opportunity to make acquaintance with that particular movement in the concert hall. From Mozart till Berlioz, there is no other music which leads us into that strange and

---

[1] Called 'Adagio' in the manuscript, but more suitably described by the 'Andante' of all printed editions.

lovely world, but a familiarity with Mozart's earlier concertos helps us to see that Girdlestone's tracing of its spiritual ancestry is not fanciful.[1]

After inspecting some dozen slow movements one cannot but acknowledge the general superiority of those which Mozart has written in lengthy, well-developed periods. It may be a fault of modern criticism to value complexity too highly, but it is difficult to be satisfied, in the middle of a fine work, with an assembly of short strophes that repeat, balance, and come to a cadence, without development. If the opening refrain of a romanza consists of eight bars, of which bars 1–2 and 5–6 are identical, and if the whole refrain occurs three times in the movement, we have to listen six times to the same melody; in an A–B–A refrain the six times becomes twelve times. In the D minor Concerto the first phrase of the Romanza appears full fourteen times, and for me the effect is a little enervating.

All generations have attested to the wonderful whole which Mozart could make out of simple materials; we have but to think of 'Là ci darem la mano'. The simplicity of this song, or of 'Vedrai carino' in the same opera, has dramatic propriety, and is cunningly set off by adjacent complexity; it is suited to the character which is being portrayed and recalls the Horatian tag *simplex munditiis*. But this is not always so. Surely Cherubino's first song, 'Non so più', is a better piece of work than the simpler, more imitative 'Voi che sapete', and even when not played with a charlatan's vagaries of tempo, the Romanza of the D minor Concerto is a tenuous piece with an allegro in the middle making the return of the refrain extra languorous.

Yet any home-pianist who cares to play over in strict time the Romanza of the C minor Concerto, K. 491, will see that Mozart, when inspired, could infuse a simple strophic movement with a wonderful inner unity. What a difference between this movement and the Romanza of K. 466! It will be noted in K. 491 that only A, of the A–B–A refrain, returns after the first departure, and that this A does not repeat within itself. The intermediate paragraphs, too, are of finer quality.

While Mozart's finest musical thought is found in sonata-andantes,

[1] I was sorely tempted to follow Girdlestone's scheme in general. This study already owes more to a reading of Girdlestone's book than I can fully acknowledge, and though conscience forbids me to alter my original approach to the andantes, I have not scrupled elsewhere to set down considerations upon this or that particular concerto which were the direct results of cogitating upon one of Girdlestone's analyses.

since their form gives scope for development of themes, not always in the middle section, the aria-form is the one in which Mozart becomes most tender and personal; he seems to find freedom while speaking in long periods. In early concertos it is difficult sometimes to label a movement either 'sonata' or 'aria'. Let us consider, for instance, the Andante of the Salzburg C major Concerto, K. 246; the binary out-lay of tonalities and the presence of a definite first subject and group of second subjects seem to show a sonata-form. On the other hand:

1. The first subject is ritornellic, being played by the orchestra before the solo repeats it.
2. The melodies are vocal in spirit, reminding us rather of a religious solo like 'Tu virginum corona' than of an individual and temperamental character-aria in opera (see Ex. 38).

A demonstration of Mozart's methods in the aria-andante needs the playing of a number of different examples, and the reader is asked to look at the notes on individual specimens (e.g. those to K. 453 or K. 482, see pages 108 and 146 ff.) and to note the immense difference between one example and another. Always, however, there is a distinction from the strophic andante, however vocal the latter may seem; this distinction is accounted for by the greater organic growth of melody, which reminds us of the ritornello-cum-jig-saw prin-ciples of a first movement. In the simple application needed for an aria, those principles were not new to Mozart; familiar instances are the solo numbers of Handel's *Messiah*, e.g. 'O thou that tellest', or 'I know that my Redeemer liveth'. To cite a familiar Mozartian parallel to the technique used in concerto andantes one can show algebraically what happens in the Countess's song 'Porgi Amor', which opens the second act of *Figaro*:

Orchestra	A (4 bars)	B C.	
Voice	A		X (4 new bars).
Orchestra	B (in dominant).		
Voice	Y.		
Orchestra	B.		

Theme A has an open end which fits orchestral B and vocal X; theme C is kept to round off the end of the whole aria after the big ritornello, just as was a lovely cadential tune in the first movement of the D minor Concerto examined above, and there is no need to go to the most mature concertos to see the emotional uses to which Mozart put his aria technique; they are perfectly demonstrated in as early a work as the B flat Concerto, K. 238.

The chief interest of Mozart's slow movements is a spiritual and not a structural one; in very few sonatas was Mozart able to use so full a range of colour and expression as in the concerto andantes; the great leaps from one 'register' to another, seen in Ex. 126, the dark tones in minor keys, the wonderful embroideries of orchestral lines by keyboard figuration, the interplay and dialogue of partners—these are fully exploited only in concertos, and had Mozart written no concertos, we might justly have regarded keyboard writing as of little interest between Bach and Beethoven, despite individual passages in the solo works of C. P. E. and W. F. Bach. Surely one is not letting fancy colour truth in declaring that the dozen best slow movements from Mozart's concertos are fit to stand beside the dozen best from all his other works, whether chamber or orchestral.[1]

(3) *Finales*

The customary finale to concertos in Mozart's day was a rondo, though there are occasional instances of sets of variations, as twice used by Mozart for his third movement. Even in early works which emulate the old *menuet galant*, the opening strophe returns in short or long rondo form. As in slow movements, Mozart does his best work when he thinks in long periods, that is to say, when he is not satisfied with the very loose and strophic form of traditional rondo.

If any critics would like to advance the theory that Mozart's best finales are those which are most serious—a theory for which there is some support, through accident and not design on Mozart's part— let them be careful not to confuse the words 'serious' and 'solemn'. If to be hilarious is to be careless in workmanship, then Haydn never wrote a fine symphony, *Idomeneo* is greater than *Figaro*, and Aristophanes and Rabelais wrote nothing to be discussed as great literature. Those who doubt that Mozart could write a great finale in which his wit fully unbuttons itself should examine the Finales of K. 449 and K. 459. It is true to say, however, that Mozart differs from Haydn, in that his finest instrumental conceptions have, on the whole, been the more serious ones, whereas Haydn's musical thinking is at its subtlest when in the highest spirits, as in the first movement of the 'Military' or the Finale of the 'Drum-roll' Symphony. It is unfortunately a fact that, in the concertos, Mozart's most frivolous rondos happen to be those which, like the Finale of K. 451 in D, are the

---

[1] Slow movements in variation form are discussed in a separate chapter dealing with Mozart's variation movements in general.

least developed and most conventional. Especially vapid is the type of Mozartian rondo in which the refrain has two sentences with a good deal of material in common, and in which both band and solo state the refrain at each of its four appearances, using little development or intricate transition work to make the returns beautiful or dramatic.

It would be easy to catalogue the various ways in which Mozart made his best rondos into more organic forms than were the simple movements of older composers such as Rameau. The refrain itself was often highly organized, as in the last concerto he wrote. An A–B–A refrain would allow variation in the allotment of its phrases between solo and orchestra, and would also make it possible for one element only, the A or the B (some refrains are further articulated), to be used in mid-movement returns. The jig-saw technique was sometimes given full play, and with A–C, A–B, B–C, B–D turning up in different places, the rondo became a thing of infinite interest and variety; or if the refrain itself had not various forms (in K. 449 the refrain enters each time in a new rhythmic dress) or, anticipating Beethoven, recked little of its traditional return to tonic harmony, Mozart might leave it as a simple skittish little tune in itself, but endow it with a rhythm capable of extended development which would bridge the full stops and commas between strophes, as in K. 459, or K. 503 with its pedal points and Bachian *bravura*. Free writing for the solo was another element which occasionally suggested itself as a source of novelty; hence K. 271, K. 482, and K. 595, each with two cadenzas. The first two of these three concertos prove conclusively that Mozart was dissatisfied with simple rondo, since they actually interrupt the movement at the point usually occupied by the third refrain in order to insert an expressive andante—a practice which is paralleled in the beautiful yet child-like C major Finale to ·K. 415, where there are two insertions of a short andante in the minor key.

Three concertos alone can be regarded as having regular sonata-rondos, viz. K. 450, K. 451, and K. 467, while the 'Coronation' Concerto, K. 537, has the shorter rondo with only three refrains. Mozart's frequent practice is to develop, in the middle of his rondo, elements taken from the refrain and from the orchestral strophe which follows the refrain. He is thus able to make an interesting transition to the point of recapitulation so that, despite the absence of the broad architecture of sonata form, an architecture based on its key relationships, the Mozartian rondo much resembles first-movement form. In general, Mozart preserves one of the older periods very distinctly, namely the point of demarcation between the refrain and the first episode. The assembly of rondo refrains having been saucily announced, always finishing with solo, whether the solo or

8. Theme 'A'

9.

10.

11. Theme 'C'

12. Theme 'D'

orchestra led off, the orchestra follows with a long and loud passage ending with a full close in the tonic key; in K. 459, one of the best rondos, this happens to be a passage of bold counterpoint, which can be made to lead in various directions for various parts of the movement. Characteristic of Mozart also is the condensation of his recapitulatory sections (as in first movements) in favour of a brilliant coda, with or without cadenza.[1]

We must not regard the rondo-finale in Mozart's hands as having much more connexion with text-book rondo than his first movements in concertos have with text-book first-movement form; and since the first of his main divisions in a rondo finale almost invariably follows a long and loud orchestral passage, coming to a full and definite close in tonic harmony, the finale begins very much as does the first movement, with the difference that piano and orchestra state their principal themes instead of organizing ritornello material. The long orchestral *forte* is, of course, ritornellic as well as thematic, as can be seen in Ex. 13, which shows the approach to the cadenza in the Finale of the D minor Concerto; but for the solo's continuation with a rondo refrain, leading to a combined solo-and-orchestral coda in the major key, this might well be an extract from the *first movement* of another D minor Concerto. Mozart's attempt to make rondo into an organic finale is most effective when the irregularities from strophic rondo are least advertised, and we cannot examine many better examples of the combined wealth and economy to be found in the best Mozartian rondos than this finale of the D minor Concerto. Its scheme is as follows:

Refrain

    A solo, 14 bars.
    A orchestra, with development, 17 bars.
    B orchestra, ritornello, forte, 33 bars. D minor.

Episode

    C solo, 10 bars.
    A both, 19 bars. C major.
    D solo, 6 bars. F minor.
    D both, with development, 37 bars. C major.
    E orchestra, 8 bars. F major.
    E solo, 8 bars.
    (Free writing for 12 bars, leading to pause on *ff* chord.)

Refrain

    A solo, 14 bars. D minor.
    A orchestra, with development, 16 bars. E major.

[1] The Rondo to K. 503 would have been much finer to modern ears had Mozart observed the practice in that instance; perhaps his full repetition was part of his general intention to maintain dignity in that particular work.

Episode

    C solo, 10 bars. A minor.
    A both, 24 bars, contrapuntally developed.
    C both, 41 bars, much interplay and modulation. A major.
    D solo, 8 bars.
    D both, with development, 21 bars.
    (This passage is brilliant for the solo and leads to a cadential shake in
    D minor; it thus sounds exactly like the finish of a first-movement
    recapitulation, and we have a surprise when the orchestra enters
    quietly. Since that entry is not made with 'A' material it cannot be
    called 'refrain'.)

Ritornello

    E orchestra, 8 bars.
    E solo, with orchestra with free *bravura* and shake in D minor, 21 bars.
    B orchestra (forte), 8 bars.
    Cadenza and coda, beginning quietly (E developed), 75 bars.
    (The coda is entirely in D major.)

The music illustrations on page 22 are labelled with the letters in
this analysis. Ex. 8 shows that a repetitive refrain is saved from dullness by an extension of its second half, thus making A asymmetrical.
Both A and D lend themselves to extension and development (Exx. 9
and 10). Theme C, on the other hand, is used rather for interplay
(Ex. 11) than for development, and is a vehicle for modulation. Contrasted with all other themes is saucy little E—the one we remember
most after a performance. How deliciously it is transformed to make
back-chat between solo and two trumpets in the coda!

The D minor Rondo is not normal—but which rondo is? When
Mozart first tackled concerto rondo, the finale was regarded as was
the minuet in a four-movement orchestral work; indeed it often was
a minuet or a piece in minuet tempo. All tensity of thought belonged
to the first movement, sentiment to the second, and complaisant
brilliance to the last. The looser and more strophic the rondo, the
more entertaining. Such a finale was rarely good enough for Mozart,
and his shade has only Mozart to blame when such a movement is not
good enough for us.

We saw that the only similarity between Mozart's concerto first-
movements and those described as 'sonata forms' in text-books lay
in their both having a broad ternary structure—an exposition ending
in dominant or relative major, a middle section, and a recapitulatory
section; similarly Mozart's best rondos ensure only one feature in
common with text-book rondo, namely a refrain which gives the
form its title.

It may seem strange that the organization of Mozart's concerto movements remained unappreciated till our own times. Tovey was ahead of German musicologists, for his essay appeared almost at the same time as Schering's generally excellent *Geschichte des Instrumentalkonzerts* (1905) wherein Mozart seems still to be accepted via Hummel. How thorough was the awakening in Germany we may judge from such a book as Ernst Bücken's *Rokoko und Klassik*, and, as usual, it is the Germans whom we have to thank for addressing themselves to textual problems as soon as the deceit of a century or more was exposed. Abert, who was Riemann's successor at Leipzig, was the first to give a whole chapter, instead of Schering's few words, to the concertos, and to show the need for a full clearance of editorial overlays; it is one task, however, to clear away Hummel's 'interpretation', and another to discern Mozart's own intentions when his autographs are incomplete.

The task of which Abert was aware, Dr. Friedrich Blume of Kiel set himself to fulfil. In his essay in the Mozart *Jahrbuch* of 1924 he shows his appreciation of the structural magnificence of the concertos, though many of us may disagree with his interpretation of Mozart's concerto conception. (Personally I see no other safe approach to this conception than by regarding the tutti as ritornelli.) But Blume gave us a far more lasting monument to his labours than is any mere book or essay. He issued pocket scores of the greatest concertos in a fully revised text, and the reader is directed both to these scores, and to Blume's introductory notes to them, in order to glean valuable commentary on (*a*) passages which the autographs leave in a sketchy condition, (*b*) the interpretation of ornaments, and (*c*) the retention of continuo functions by the pianist in non-solo passages. (Eulenburg miniature scores of K. 365, 450, 453, 466, 467, 482, 488, 491, 503, 537, 595.)

In one point we may allow ourselves to differ from the German scholars. By them the former attitude to the concertos which regarded them, even in Schering's book, as fashionable music for an evening's entertainment, is now deplored; I do not think that attitude was mistaken. Despite the earnestness of purpose, the tragic atmosphere, of one or two very exceptional concertos and movements, the concerto in Mozart's hands remained brilliant, fashionable, entertaining. Greatness and solemnity must not be regarded as inseparable companions, and Schering's remark need not offend one who deeply appreciates the subtlety and high organization of the concertos.

CHAPTER III

THE ANCESTRY. KEYBOARD CONCERTOS BEFORE MOZART

In his fifth deal of 'Brandenburg' instruments, Bach raises the continuo player to chief performer. It is notable that the bass of the harpsichord part is figured only where the right hand stave is empty; it is therefore probable that the functions of Cembalo Concertato and Cembalo Continuo were invested in one keyboard; it is also possible, but not probable, that Mozart's audiences remembered seeing a

continuo player doing his duty even when a clavier soloist was to the forefront. Mozart's clavier remembers its humble origin, though its memory fades until in the last three concertos it sometimes fails to provide its own bass. But in Mozart solo and orchestra are in mutual liaison. It is mistaken to declare that, in concerto, Beethoven set the orchestra free. He set the piano free—so free that players long for support while practising. The Mozartian performer, doubling orchestral bass as he should when not playing a concertante section, rattling away in memory of Domenico Alberti, or arpeggiating orchestral harmony, is not an accompanied soloist; he is sparring partner to the band. His part never anticipates that of the Grieg Concerto, which one can play at home quite happily without a pocket orchestra or a second piano.

Grieg, Schumann, and others each wrote a *piano concerto*; Mozart wrote concertos for piano and orchestra, but they came from a form not unlike that to which concerto returned. Bach's home-players, with or without the luxury of an octave-coupler, imitated the solo and tutti-ritornello of a concerto grosso every time they tackled a work like the 'Italian' Concerto. In the 'Brandenburg' Concertos we see a series of variations upon the partners. Nos. 3 and 6 are normal concerti grossi in which a small group of strings opposes the tutti; of the other four, No. 5 would stand out as the first clavier concerto well known to modern listeners but for the fact that solo flute and solo fiddle are grouped with the cembalo concertato, which also remains continuo. But the great cadenzas which let us hear the clavier by itself emphasize the fact that flute and fiddle could be omitted. Bach's innovating turn of genius was of the type to exalt the humble and meek time-keeper with dignity; Haydn would have turned the surprise into a joke.

One hesitates to admit that Bach took the turning which, nearly thirty years later, produced the most complicated of instrumental forms. None of his concertos including a clavier, or known to have done so in its original form, brings us any nearer to Mozart than does the fifth 'Brandenburg'. Even the well-known D minor Concerto of Bach, whose figuration shows it to have been originally conceived for the violin, leaves the ritornello principle at the same stage as in the tuttis of a concerto grosso; in other words, there is no high organization of ritornello materials; the tutti remains all-of-a-piece, as it does in the various violin concertos by men like Vivaldi, several of which Bach arranged as keyboard concertos. We find the rough 'six sections' of the diagrams in Chapter I among the violin concertos of the Italian virtuosi immediately preceding the age of Bach and Handel. Like the 'Brandenburg' Concertos, these works rarely use any themes for the solo or solo-group which cannot be traced in the opening tutti.

Their parent, and therefore the grandparent of the classical concerto, was the operatic aria. To supply a voracious demand the Venetians of the early eighteenth century (Albinoni, Vivaldi, and the Marcello brothers) wrote many operas, i.e. hundreds of ritornello arias. Imagine familiar examples, such as arias in *Messiah* or Bach's Passions, with oboes or violins replacing voices. We thus imagine brisk or pathetic movements of the type used by Venetian composers after *c.* 1710 and emulated by German court and church composers later. The classical concerto owes only contrast of texture to the concerto grosso associated with Corelli and Handel, shaped like a baroque suite or sonata with no precise number of movements. The three-movement works, of which Vivaldi's had most influence, made popular the virtuosity of solo instrumentalists. As far as is known, they had to await the Bach family for the solo advancement of the harpsichord. The clavier concerto became fashionable in London and Vienna in the 1770s just as the fortepiano was replacing the harpsichord in concert rooms. The boy Mozart's models were the concertos of his friend J. C. Bach in London. He may also have been influenced by the violin concertos of Viotti, his slightly older contemporary. Viotti travelled much, but was notably acclaimed in Paris and London.

The epithet *galant* is the musical equivalent of 'rococo', and is applied to the graceful, mannered euphony of the serenade and divertimento, fashionable in public, semi-public, or courtly music-makings of mid-eighteenth century. The *galant* style soon made the clavier useful and concertos fashionable, for keyboard figurations could supply all the hey-diddle-diddle busy-ness which prevented compositions in that style from being too homophonic, too enervated. Arpeggios and running passages could decorate unambitious melody, give brilliance to lengthy periods of smiling melody, add rhythmic interest to simple harmonic texture without further complicating it, and beautify commonplace structure with a wealth of florid and equally commonplace ornament, much of which was supplied by the performer, such supply being indeed regarded as a skilled accomplishment of his profession. Even Mozart's concertos may have had a very different clavier part in certain places from what is offered in those places to-day, and it is amusing to imagine that endearing snob Dittersdorf making his safe and obsequious reply to the emperor's inquiry as to whether Clementi or Mozart were the better performer: 'Sire, the one plays with art; the other with art and taste'. That criticism may have had more precision for contemporary readers than for us.

Two qualities of the *galant* style must be emphasized: first *it was a definite style*, capable of developments simply because of its limitations; secondly it was an excellent medium for Mozart's concerto conceptions, because it opened a wide field of interest for those engaged in devising interplay of strings with a florid solo part. This may be enough to explain how we find Mozart in direct succession to *galant* concertists like Wagenseil, Schobert, and Christian Bach, rather than in the train of a far more profound and interesting musical personality like Carl Philip Emanuel Bach, whose concertos should be heard to-day, since they would considerably surprise musicians who are familiar only with his sonatas.

C. P. E. Bach seems to be one of those artists who have tremendous ideas and who strive hard to express them while being fettered by the lack of one gift—a consistent, developed style. He wrote fifty-six clavier concertos, some of which enable the ritornello to be shortened, others of which bring the ritornello three or four times into a first movement *en bloc* like the refrain of a rondo, except that C. P. E.'s refrain appears in all sorts of keys. Intermediate sections show considerable development and a wealth of thematic materials, but no architecture of keys to satisfy those with symmetrical pre-conceptions. There is great diversity of form, and an unusual varia-tion in the number of movements between one concerto of Emanuel Bach and another. What is the analyst to make of his C minor Concerto (Wot. 43. 2)? It offers four complete movements, being therefore unique among eighteenth-century concertos; the only move-ment in a major key is the third, a minuet in E flat. Each movement leads dramatically into the next without full cadences, and the C minor refrain, which makes the first movement into a vast rondo, comes again several times with similar effect in the last movement.[1]

Here, then, is a work anticipating Liszt's one-movement concep-tions, but what the prejudiced ear misses in any one section, either in this or in other concertos of Emanuel Bach, is anything correspond-ing with the ternary 'middle section'. The music of individual para-graphs may be developed and extended by long thinking which is more potent than any amount of technical jugglery of the kind called 'development' by examiners for musical diplomas. The Concertos in F minor,[2] C minor, and D minor (Wot. 23) are greater works than any symphony from his pen, and show something in common with the music of his father. Ex. 15 is taken from the prelude to the first named of these works; the mild discords and feminine cadences remind us of English cathedral composers of the period, but the sentiment is highly individual when we consider that the concerto was *the galant* member of the larger forms, and the one in which display was expected.

C. P. E. Bach housed and taught his younger brother, Johann Christian, the Benjamin of Sebastian's sons, who later studied in Italy before making London his performing and publishing head-quarters. J. C. Bach's letters to Padre Martini are full of a genuine

---

[1] Prof. Girdlestone has recently informed me of a four-movement concerto by Father Antonio Soler, organist and court composer at the Escorial. Of his six concertos, two have been broadcast by the B.B.C. as piano quintets.

[2] Not in Wotquenne's catalogue. See *John Christian Bach* by Sanford Terry.

gratitude which makes us forget what the writer owed to his influential brother; amongst that elder brother's several concerto styles is one almost as *galant* as Johann Christian's, though more intricate and nervous; even so, any movement, or paragraph, may shift suddenly into a type of sentiment which cannot be regarded as conceding anything to contemporary taste. We see this in a fine Concerto in D major, the Andante of which is written in alternations of E minor and E major, the orchestra making a refrain in the former key to punctuate various solo departures in the latter (Exs. 16a and 16b).

Whether by accident or design, young Mozart came under a very different influence from that of Emanuel Bach, and however vapid the immediate ancestry of Mozart's concertos seems to-day, the *concerto galant* had a destiny; the *sinfonia galante* had not, neither had the grandiose experiments of Emanuel Bach, whose concertos, nevertheless, should be given in their own right the performances for which they are long overdue. A powerful harpsichord should be used.

It is convenient to isolate four centres of concerto activity during Mozart's infancy—Mannheim, Vienna, Paris, and London; we make no further note of Mannheim, which is overshadowed by the huge figure of C. P. E. Bach; as for Vienna, it is curious that Mozart was little influenced by the school which flourished at the capital nearest his home. At the age of six, he is known to have played a concerto by Wagenseil before the Austrian court, the composer turning over for him. The concertos of the Vienna, Paris, and London groups are all of the *galant* type, and only those of the London musicians have a melodic grace and a complaisant vitality which merit an occasional performance to-day. Wagenseil, the court composer, was doyen of the Vienna concertists. He included his pupils Steffan, Hoffman, and, of course, Haydn. Specimens of their work are to be found in the British Museum, and poor stuff it is; Haydn's excels Wagenseil's only in its tunes. Haydn wrote twenty-four concertos of which two, in D and G, are available in modern editions. The man who prunes the D major to sonata dimensions can provide himself with a merry party piece, and I should not call him a Philistine.

The Paris virtuosi were nearly all migrant Germans, of whom Schobert is the most worthy of consideration as a composer. His concertos are no great matter, though they have first movements in the Mozartian 'six sections'; his sonatas contain better music, which evidently attracted the attention of the Mozarts on their Paris visits, since young Wolfgang's first 'concertos' are arrangements of sonata movements by Schobert and his associates, Raupach and Honauer;

the sonatas are converted from three movements to six by orchestral ritornelli extracted from the solo sections. (Wyzewa and Saint-Foix show that Mozart's first sets of keyboard variations were modelled on

15. C.P.E.BACH. F mi. Concerto. [Not in Wotquenne]

16 (a) C.P.E.BACH. Concerto in D. [Wot. 43. ii.] Andante.

(b)

those found in sonatas by Eckhardt and Honauer.)

In the hands of the London school, the *concerto galant* is a thing of beauty, however slender. Did we not know of Wolfgang's affection for his genial friend 'London Bach', we should suspect his knowledge of Johann Christian's concertos from the close similarities between Mozart's immature keyboard writing and Bach's. It is a mistake to exaggerate similarities of *style*, and those who dislike Mozart's earlier compositions make themselves ridiculous by declaring that certain formulae 'could have been written by any dozen of his contemporaries'. There is all the difference in the world between first-class and third-class Mozart, but the more one sees of the contemporaries of Mozart and Haydn, the more one recognizes that, between them, those two used a musical vocabulary shared by few other men, although Dittersdorf may sometimes be mistaken for one of them. We know the standard technique of that age almost exclusively through Haydn and Mozart, whose similarities of style are more remarkable than the obvious differences, especially in view of the fact that few great contemporaries have had such radically different natures and interests. Moreover, the resemblances are not confined to their poorer music; whole phrases of fine Haydn could pass for fine Mozart, but nobody needs the insight of a Saint-Foix to reject, as specimens of Mozart, the extracts from J. C. Bach's A major Concerto, quoted at Ex. 17.

Of far more interest than Mozart's stylistic resemblances to J. C. Bach are his developments of structural principles clearly established in the concertos of his London friend. In Ex. 17a we have the prelude to a first movement which will utilize the partial or short ritornello (marked A) as well as the full ritornelli at sections 3 and 6. The passage marked B should be compared with Ex. 17b, which shows the solo using the same starting-point and then taking its own course, in aria tradition; the opening phrase is thus both principal subject and principal ritornello. Ex. 17c shows another important usage of the London concertists; it is a solo subject which has not been heard upon the orchestra, but is new to the solo exposition. We have seen to what lengths Mozart enriched the solo exposition with new material, thereby making ritornelli the more effective. Peters issues a very good specimen of J. C. Bach's art as a concertist, one of a set of six concertos first published by John Welcker of London in 1777; in the January of that year Mozart wrote his first great Concerto, K. 271 in E flat, though the previous Salzburg concertos are fit to stand beside any of Christian Bach's. A comparison of Bach's best-known concerto, that in B flat (op. 13, no. 4), with Mozart's E flat[1] will show how much Mozart at the age of twenty-one had outstripped a concertist who happened to be exactly twice his age. The difference is that between genius and great talent, though one can take too seriously J. C. Bach's remark: 'My brother (C. P. E.) lives to compose; I compose to live.'

The form in which many pre-Mozartian concertos were published may do them something less than justice. Publishers issued parts which made the works accessible to the smallest salon combination; hence the broadcast of a concerto by Soler under the misnomer 'Piano Quintet in C'; parts happened to be available for minimum orchestra, and ducal establishments rarely had *normal resident* orchestras which would need more than one desk, i.e. one part-copy, for each string 'voice'. Two or three first fiddles might share one desk and the bass player might overlook the figured continuo part.[2] Thompson's or Welcker's title-pages for the J. C. Bach concertos are typical: 'A Third Sett of Six Concertos for the Harpsichord or Piano-Forte, with Accompaniments for two Violins and a Bass, two Hautboys and Two French Horns ad Libitum.' Huberty of Paris and Artaria of Vienna issued 'favourite' works with the same commendation, which does not speak for enterprise in the wind parts, still less in the missing viola parts; a special feature of Mozart's orchestral technique is his gradual raising of the viola-player's status from that of Muggins, who made third-part harmony or else doubled the bass at the octave, to that of W. A. Mozart, who gave himself, as violist, as expressive and essential a part as he did to Dittersdorf, Haydn, and Vanhall, the other members of his Sunday morning quartet. The importance of this raising of interest within the string texture is well shown in J. Arthur Watson's essay 'Mozart and the Viola', in vol. xxii, no. 1 of *Music and Letters*.

Burney tells us that the music of John Baptist Vanhall, or Wanhal, 1739–1813, a musician of Dutch extraction born in Bohemia, became well known in England before that of Haydn, though Vanhall was the younger man. He studied under Dittersdorf and must have known Haydn. His output was enormous, and as no modern editions are yet available I quote the themes of a sample Clavier Concerto in D. Its structure and style show close resemblance to those of Christian Bach and young Mozart. Ex. 18*a* opens the concerto, being principal subject and principal ritornello; Ex. 18*b* continues the orchestral prelude and remains orchestral, i.e. ritornellic, throughout the movement; Ex. 18*c* is the new keyboard theme for the solo exposition and remains such, while yet a second 'new' solo theme, Ex. 18*d*, opens the middle section.

Other members of the London school were, like J. C. Bach, migrant Germans, such as Bach's partner in concert-giving, C. F.

---

[1] Of recent years K. 271 has been given many more performances than either of its brothers in E flat; the reasons for its comparative popularity are probably those I have described in a different connexion later.

[2] For further details see Adam Carse's *The Orchestra in the Eighteenth Century*.

Abel (1725–87) and J. S. Schröter (1750–88), who succeeded Bach as music teacher to the English royal family. One of Mozart's letters expresses admiration for Schröter's concertos, though they seem even less interesting than those of Bach and Vanhall.

17 (a)   J.C.BACH. Concerto in A.

(b)

(c)

18 (a)   Vanhall. Concerto in D.

(b)

(c)

(d)

Such was the concerto as accepted by Mozart, and we may recognize how much he established its principles, while nurturing it towards a richer and nobler maturity, when we reflect that even its three-movement form was not finally consolidated by the London group. There are plenty of two-movement concertos by J. C. Bach, the second movement being a minuet or minuet-rondo in distinct, undeveloped strophes, or sometimes a set of variations. Mozart's Salzburg concertos rarely stray from the normal plan: First movement—Andante (binary sonata)—Rondo. His rondos, even in Salzburg days, show the first sproutings and prunings which were later to give unity and dramatic force to his best finales, and it would be possible to demonstrate with another set of examples, taken from last instead of first movements, that the only important history of the Mozartian conception of concerto is to be traced through the works of the master himself.

They begin with K. 175 in D, the very scoring of which marks it from previous essays in concerto. The arrangements from J. C. Bach's sonatas were scored for two violins and a bass (K. 107), to which a clavecin gave sufficient opposition or, as *clavier continuo*, support. The arrangements from the 'Parisian Germans' (K. 37, 39–41) use full strings, together with a pair of horns and of oboes; but even these could be countered by whatever type of solo instrument a town happened to provide when the Mozarts halted there. But K. 175 in D, with its trumpets, drums, and full orchestra, needs the piano, so perfect a partner and opponent to a symphonic force that Mozart recognized its superiority over all wind and string instruments for use in concerto. He renounced the other instruments in its favour, and he ceased to write piano concertos only when he ceased to follow the career of public pianist and concertist.

It should be pointed out that all the great clavier concertos of Mozart were intended for the piano. Readers who wish to examine the evidence are referred to an essay by Nathan Broder in the American *Musical Quarterly* of October 1941, which makes it clear that the harpsichord was not used by Mozart for K. 414 or any subsequent clavier concerto.

CHAPTER IV

MOVEMENTS IN VARIATION FORM

OF all movements longer than a song or dance, the set of variations is the most democratic, for the simple can follow its high roads while the musically learned investigate its subtleties. In a variety entertainment a set of easy but showy variations gets applause from both the impressed and the amused; queues for Queen's Hall concerts in pre-war days had many a copper charmed from them by a great natural artist, an unshaven Haydn called Old Moke, whose virtuosity upon the penny-whistle reached its climax with a set of variations on 'Pop goes the Weasel'.

There are almost the same limitations to Mozart's sets of piano variations; indeed, Mozart is less recherché than Moke, and that is one of the reasons for august dicta upon his 'poor contribution to the list of great works in variation form'. There is a great gulf between the Old Mokery of 'The King's Hunt', 'The Carman's Whistle', the chaconnes of the French Grand Epoch, 'The Harmonious Blacksmith', or even the 'Goldberg' Variations with Proper Pride peeping behind the technical descriptions which precede some of their numbers, and the intimate expression which Beethoven found in variation form during his last years. It would be useless to pretend that Mozart bridges that gulf were his claim based upon the various sets of keyboard variations; yet Mozart does bridge the gulf, while belonging always to the Old Moke school; and the keystone of his bridge is set among the six quartets dedicated to Haydn.

It will be remembered that Mozart interrupted their composition (after he had finished the second, in D minor) with a set of variations which showed new and wonderful sensibility. The following year, 1784, is a remarkable one; it has a beginning and an end without parallel, but its middle shows a summer vacation, at least from composition. In March–April Mozart wrote the Concertos K. 449–51, and then, on 12 April, completed the G major Concerto, K. 453, with its last movement in variation form. No lengthy work came from his pen till September, on the thirtieth of which he was ready with his B flat Concerto for the blind pianist, Maria Thérèse von Paradies. It contains what I think Mozart's most beautiful but not most advanced set of variations. Between this Concerto, K. 456, and the previous G major are only two Köchel numbers, one the Violin Sonata in B flat and the other a set of variations! Moreover, the variations are Mozart's finest set for piano solo, those on the song 'Unser dummer Pöbel meint' from Gluck's *Pilgrims of Mecca*.

Even more important than the abnormal number of works with variations is the resuming of the 'Haydn' Quartets (after his most imposing Piano Sonata, that in C minor) with an exhibition of new technical procedures which must be reckoned remarkable. First comes the so-called 'Hunt' Quartet in B flat; then the A major so admired by Beethoven that he copied it in score. Its slow movement is a set of variations ranked among Mozart's deepest utterances in the form. But this is not all. The two quartets show feats of constructional virtuosity in other movements. The first movement of the B flat germinates from a single theme, as does that of the 'Haffner' Symphony; this may have been a compliment to Haydn, who commonly made use of the practice. The A major Finale is packed with brilliant and lucid counterpoint, which drew Beethoven's chief interest in the work. If no eminent musicologist has yet traced its influence upon Beethoven's own A major Quartet, op. 18, no. 5, he has yet opportunity.

What have such movements to do with variation form? Any movements affect a composer's use of variation form if they show a new interest in the treatment of themes, and not just artistry in organizing a mass of small material—an artistry of which Mozart was already master. To him variations were a chance to exhibit virtuosity of treatment; even in the C minor Concerto he remained a member of the Old Moke school and not a founder of the Beethoven-Brahms dynasty. It cannot be too much stressed that, had Mozart and Beethoven been exact contemporaries, they would have shown different, not rival, turns of genius; harm is done by measuring Mozart's introspective works by spiritual values which his great successor brought into the ascendant. (In this connexion see discussion of the D minor Concerto in Chapter XIII.) Beethoven showed a new love for variation form when he came to his last mystical phase of writing; was this to exhibit virtuosity? Impossible; such a reason might have been advanced in the days of the 'Kreutzer' Sonata, but not at the end. More sensible is the argument that Beethoven wanted

to feel a universal response to his music, and that the same sentiments
which are voiced in the 'Ode to Heavenly Joy' urged him to use the
form which puts least strain upon the musically simple. Surely,
though, Beethoven's chief interest in variations came from the fact
that, as viewed by him, they called *less* for virtuosity of thematic
treatment than for the most direct spiritual communication music
had yet borne. They made him free, and the depth of his inspiration
defeated technical virtuosity by pushing technique almost beyond the
limits of practical performance.

Mozart was neither man nor musician of that kind. He was a
specialist professional musician, to whom depth of thought meant
virtuosity of music. His mentality was not of the order which produced Brahms's 'St. Anthony' set or Beethoven's 'Waltz of Diabelli'
set, each member of which has a distinct character of its own.
Brahms's finest passages, even in symphonies, are lyrical; tremendous
industry and self-criticism gave him ability to deal with long forms,
but his inspiration is more obvious and spontaneous in songs and in
the exquisite pianoforte intermezzi. Brahms is therefore most happy'
in a form, that of variations, which consists of a series of small pieces,
each with its own conception. For all the good songs in *The Magic
Flute*, Mozart's greatest genius was shown in long edifices, such as
the second act of *Figaro*, the Kyrie of the C minor Mass, or the first
movement of the C minor Concerto, all constructed from a wealth of
small pieces. 'Porgi Amor' might be the opening of a slow symphonic
movement; 'Non so più' opens with the rhythm of the G minor
symphony and might have been built into its rival; the opening of
'Voi che sapete' or 'Vedrai carino' could be that of a wind serenade;
and how easily another 'Paris' or 'Haffner' Symphony could have
begun as does the last act of *Don Giovanni*, just before 'Già la mensa
preparata'! By nature Mozart was the man to put his personal
imprint not on variations but on the complex forms of operatic
scena and concerto.

Yet there is a marked change in the quality of his variations after
1784. It was certainly a busman's holiday he took that summer; what
were his studies? More of the Bach and Handel he had come to love
at Van Swieten's music-makings? Haydn? Perhaps it was of these
months that he thought when he wrote: 'There is scarcely a famous
master whose works I have not carefully and diligently studied.'
A short scrutiny of all Mozart's essays in variation form will show
that the presence of non-keyboard instruments usually brings an abnormal improvement in quality. The Old Mokes of his boyhood

included two clavier virtuosi, Eckhardt and Honauer, whose sonatas ending with variations he came to know as a lad in Paris; Wyzewa and Saint-Foix, who give this information (although Leopold's letters to his friend Hagenauer in Salzburg are the chief source), also suppose that Mozart's habit of including a slow or minor-key variation was imitated from the practice of performers whom he met in Mannheim. The nine or ten sets of keyboard variations which date from before the Vienna period were saved from banality, first by the quality of their figuration, many an example of which was reflected in concertos and sonatas by the natural selection of Mozart's memory, secondly by the inclusion of variations in a minor key which gave that slight challenge of the unfamiliar which always brought out the best from Mozart's conservative nature.

Now I do not assert that there is any great intellectuality or spirituality (blessed word!) about the early piano variations; they are just better Old Mokery than the Older Mokes gave. Nor is there any sudden access of inspiration in later solo sets which Mozart added to their number. Several allusions in letters show that he set no great store by them, that their writing was often a hindrance to more serious composition, but that they were a very present help in material trouble. They made neat compliments as presents and, almost alone among composers' wares in those days, brought immediate money by return. To do this they had to be largely what their recipients wanted them to be. The tune was a 'favourite air', or the simulation of one, which the purchasers liked to have buzzing in their heads; the variations were just sufficient to enable the same dish to be re-served palatably. Mozart, though never attempting to serve a dish of different food, could add a piquant sauce. The variations on airs had themselves to be airy, and if, in minor-key variations, a character appeared not akin in spirit to the air, aberration was clearly corrected in the next variation.

Considering these limitations, Mozart's keyboard variations do not compare unfavourably with those by Haydn in the G and E flat Sonatas, which were not necessarily bound to please, and which, if they show greater departure from the theme, as do some Purcell chaconnes, have not greater artistry than Mozart showed in the actual keyboard writing. Haydn's F minor set is exceptional. Nobody but a crank would call Mozart's sets great music, but it is hard to understand why they should be despised while the colourless set from the A major Sonata is admired. Max Reger's dressing of the little A major 'Cradle Song' in cope, mitre, rings, and gauntlets is not offensive; for even *if* Mozart wrote the tune, it is obvious that Reger took far more pleasure in his variations than did Mozart in his own set.

The clavier began as a plaything in rich and royal households. Not every great personage who helped pass time tinkling upon spinet or virginals had a markedly musical nature. As for the professional musicians, is it to be supposed that the composer of the Mass for Five Voices unburdened his soul for the new toy in the Old Mokish strains of 'The Carman's Whistle'? To know Byrd's treatment of a theme, we hear his choral masterpieces; to know the best Mozart variations, we look in the 'Haydn' Quartets, the Clarinet Quintet, the Serenade for Thirteen Wind Instruments, and above all, the piano concertos. Even in the concertos the piano keeps to its traditional embroideries, as it does in many a movement which does not profess to be a set of variations.

In 1784 Mozart began his *Verzeichnis*, or thematic-note-book-catalogue of all his works. Its first pages were rich in entries of pieces using variation form. They are headed by the three Piano Concertos, K. 449, 450, 451, of March–April. The second of these is the brilliant Concerto in B flat whose slow movement is a set of variations, though not usually acknowledged as such. It may well be studied along with the slow movement of the next B flat Concerto, K. 456, written for Mlle. Paradies, since the themes and treatments have something in common. They are very different from the themes first announced by the clavier and intended for use in finales in the G major and C minor Concertos, K. 453 and 491. In Ex. 21 will be seen the openings of these variation themes intended for finales, together with their ancestor, 'Ah, vous dirai-je, Maman!' Their repeated notes and simple harmony, using only one or two chords per bar, show the kind of melody chosen for virtuosic treatment. Very different are the singing orchestral andantes quoted just above them; these intrinsically beautiful tunes are not met in keyboard variations, and with them Mozart has no intention of making variations of great independence. The tunes are too lovely to alter; their very cadences seem to recur throughout the slow movements for which they are chosen. In K. 450 (see Ex. 20) we would fain hear the tune more than we do in the three presentations and coda, for English ears have been used to variations of this kind from Dowland's 'Lachrymae' to Delius's *Brigg Fair*, and the quotation made on page 88, Ex. 75, will show that a comparison of *Brigg Fair* with a piece from Mozart is not far-fetched.

Nevertheless there are only two of these 'English' variation-sets in the mature concertos; they must be regarded as meditations upon the theme rather than as Brahmsian transformations of it, and they recall Shelley's 'vibrates in the memory'. Especially is this true of the

19.

second of their instances, the G minor Andante of K. 456. Here is one of Mozart's most lovely tunes; indeed I know no lovelier in its particular mood, and it seems desirable to digress a little in the examination of that mood. Musicians to-day find a poignance in the G minor quintet, the G minor symphony, and tunes like the one we are examining (Ex. 19), which was not noted by Schumann who saw only 'Hellenic grace' in the symphony. Yet Schumann was as sensitive a man as any one of us, and we must be careful not to believe

every suggestion we read about the pathetic state of Mozart's soul
when he penned a tune in the minor key. The subjective reactions of

our own age to Mozart's seemingly introspective tunes may be more
fair to Mozart than were those of Schumann's time, but Mozart's
shade may have a wicked grin upon its face sometimes. This G minor
tune of K. 456, which brings tears to modern eyes, is not so very
unlike Barbarina's little song in the last act of *Figaro*; it, too, may be

all about a lost pin. Was Mozart content to extend the mood of the tune up to five variations and coda, or was he voicing the sentiments of his audience at the 'Affecting Spectacle' of the blind Paradies, the

lovely soul in its dark house? It is wiser, surely, to err on the side of reticence than to add to the pile of writing about Mozart's introspection. Yet the mood may be fully subjective. We cannot imagine the loneliness of the greatest natural genius known to musicians, nor the bewilderment of one whose mind was developed musically to an enormous disparity with other developments. He must have felt deeply the need of a companion who had more in common with him than had any of his immediate acquaintance. Moreover, none of the older masters gave expression to the mood observed in this G minor tune except Mozart; Beethoven's sorrow or anger is as exhilarating as his joy, for those are active passions; Mozart rarely voiced them except in operatic passages like the arias for the Queen of Night; and the conventional form which taste and conviction forced upon him made his introspective works far more poignant than are the free tears of later artists.

The insistence on one mood in K. 456 is remarkable. A murderous dissection of the tune is, for once, of some value. If we look at it bar by bar, we see laid before us the whole technique of grief:

1. A complaint, three times made.
2. The obvious possibility of a descending chromatic bass to it.
3. The false consolation of a major cadence.
4. Phrases which follow it, first in D minor with a pathetic sforzando, second in C minor with a weary rise and fall, introduced by chromatic part-writing.
5. Two short cries, with questioning silences.
6. Abandonment to G minor.
7. A masterly extension of the tune, emphasizing the chromatics and repeating the G minor cadence.

If incidental music be needed to the story of an invalid's sleepless night, here it is at its most beautiful. The very features noted above are those which the variations emphasize—the chromatics multiply, the sforzandi are intensified, the silences are retained, and the piano writing approaches a Chopin *spianato* passage (see Exx. 22 and 24).

There are five variations, the second, third, and fourth being doubles, that is to say each half is varied or decorated first by the orchestra and then by the piano, which may or may not be accompanied. The penultimate variation is in the relative major, but the lachrymose nature of the whole movement is established again both by the last, fifth variation, and by a coda of haunting beauty whose length is that of a sixth variation.

Of an entirely different order are the two virtuosic sets of variations used as finales. The kind of theme chosen for these movements has been noted, but after inspecting the G minor Variations of K. 456, we should also observe two particular aspects of Mozart's writing in the finale of the G major Concerto, K. 453, and the C minor, K. 491. They are:

1. A very different type of scoring.
2. The infusion of contrapuntal ingenuity.

Both these elements lead to another, that of capricious and nimble invention; while not straying too far from his themes, Mozart seeks contrast in these variations which he did not want in K. 456, with its 'English' treatment. Two obvious ways of combining continuity with fairly close adherence to the theme are instrumental change and contrapuntal decoration. Mozart's ability to vary slightly while embellishing considerably are shown in treatments of the C minor theme at Exx. 25, 26, and 27.

He knew his audience. The variation finale had to be as popular as the rondo finale, pleasing the musically simple while interesting himself and the musically advanced. The double variations gave continuous opportunity to contrast the theme in its simplicity with immediate pianistic or orchestral elaboration. In both the G major and the C minor Concertos the first variation is extremely simple; it is also a single variation for the piano alone (Exx. 28a and 28b). Even so, Mozart cautiously recalls the theme before varying it a second time, a treatment made possible by the 'double' feature. The first half is given out simply, the only novelty being that it sounds through woodwind tone; then the solo makes brilliant variation (Ex. 29).

Of the remaining variations, only one or two are of any boldness. There is room in the G major set only for one big departure which coincides with the variation in the relative minor. There is no other instance in all Mozart's writing of the wonderful technique used here. The band gives 'fourth species' in each half, and the solo at its entry makes the syncopations doubly nervous, with movement at the minim, the crotchet, the quaver (Ex. 30). Still more remarkable are the contrasts in tone colour made by jumps from one part of the keyboard to the other (Ex. 31). The strong correction of a variation with wide aberration from the theme is noticed in the sets for solo keyboard as well as in the concertos, though the solo sets are denied the correction possible in a double variation. Other old keyboard devices which appear in the concertos are the variation with triplets, bass or soprano, corresponding with the march-variation, and the type with running scales for the bass.

When using scales or triplets, Mozart is much more self-critical than his contemporaries, with whom these procedures do not always arrive on a harmony note without occasional skips; some composers make their 'wangles' difficult, ugly, or patent. Mozart always contrives to make them logical and grateful to the hand. A type of variation notably absent from the solo keyboard sets is that employing counterpoint of the quality seen in Ex. 32.

A good final variation is an artistic necessity. What happens in the
G major Concerto is discussed later; suffice it here to say that

Mozart ends his movement in the spirit of opera buffa. The C minor
Concerto uses a conventional practice in a very unconventional way.
The favourite method of changing from duple to triple or compound
time at the end of a rondo, usually to 6/8, is used to bring out all the
pathetic elements in the theme. That theme has appeared dignified,
tranquil, playful, magniloquent, martial, tearful, and stormy, but so

that we shall not leave it with its part greater than its whole—with our minds set upon its pathetic transformation in 6/8—Mozart ends with a brusque and highly 'classical' rush of strings on the minor scale. The whole movement is clinched and its classical unity enhanced by that artistic stroke.

But the great 6/8 final variation is an elegiac masterpiece; the Neapolitan Sixth, which previously coloured half a bar of the theme, now occupies the first half of two bars, and in the fantasia that follows there seem to be as many Neapolitan Sixths as there are common chords; chromatics abound in the melodic variation and in the harmonies. What a pity that there are but two concerto finales in variation form!

CHAPTER V

THE SALZBURG CONCERTOS

THE Salzburg trumpeter Schachtner, friend of the Mozart family, tells how Leopold Mozart examined some ink blobs made by his child, and was astonished at the 'correct observance of rules'; Wolfgang was four years old and declared that he was writing a concerto for clavecin. This fact proves that he had grown up in a world wherein clavecin concertos were familiar, though the boy knew more of the concert world than of other fields of musical activity. The concerto was the form *par excellence* for a fashionable concert; sonatas were home music in those days, and the composer who wished to shine in a public concert had to be a performer, so that in the concerto he fulfilled his public obligation of double virtuoso. At the age of nine, while still in London, Mozart framed three of J. C. Bach's sonatas with orchestral ritornelli and called them concertos. Two years later he gave Salzburg audiences four such works from his pen, and until recently they were thought to be his own compositions. Wyzewa and Saint-Foix have identified most of their movements with those of sonatas by German virtuosi whose place of performance and publication was Paris, in which city the boy's parents may have obtained copies for him. We know that he wrote sets of variations modelled upon those of Eckhardt and Honauer, and by accepting the authority of Erwin Bodky and Alfred Einstein for the origin of one movement not traced by the French biographers, and Blom's suggestion that the second movement of K. 37 may be original, we can tabulate the movements of these first four 'Mozart' concertos thus:

1. K. 37, Concerto in F   (*a*) Raupach.
                                    (*b*) Mozart (?).
                                    (*c*) Honauer.
2. K. 39, Concerto in B flat (*a*) Raupach.
                                    (*b*) Schobert.
                                    (*c*) Raupach.
3. K. 40, Concerto in D   (*a*) Honauer.
                                    (*b*) Eckhardt.
                                    (*c*) C. P. E. Bach (Bodky and Einstein).
4. K. 41, Concerto in G   (*a*) Honauer.
                                    (*b*) Raupach.
                                    (*c*) Raupach.

They are works of slight build with clavecin acting both as solo and continuo, the distinction not always being clear.[1] Though the solo exposition is longer than the prelude, from which Mozart omits development and passage-work, it has no new theme. The middle section is lengthened and the attempt to give concerto proportions by inserting a coda at the conclusion of Raupach's sonata is not very well contrived; the addition sticks like mother's extra piece of pastry on the last pie. I have examined the Raupach sonatas and do not indulge fancy by declaring that Mozart's alterations, though slight, all tend to heighten sentiment. Ex. 33 compares two openings. Mozart's additions are made plain by a diagram in which all sections are drawn to scale, with the additional matter enclosed in thick lines.

Orchestral prelude	A a	B
First ritornello	A	Coda
Middle section	C	
Recapitulation	A a	B	Scales, &c.
Final ritornello	A	Solo	Coda

Exposition: A a | B |

Though so much shorter than the corresponding sections of later Mozart concertos, the units in these youthful works have the same relative sizes; there is not the wealth of themes, nor any high organization of them—not even the new theme or themes for solo exposition and middle section found in Vanhall, Christian Bach, and the London group.

Mozart's first original concerto remained a favourite for some time, both with its composer, who brought it out anew when he first went to Vienna, and with his public, whose delight in it is mentioned in letters. This D major Concerto, K. 175, was written in December 1773, when Mozart was eighteen. Alone among the Salzburg concertos it uses trumpets and drums, which may have increased its popularity. It is a brave affair which shows the first requisite of any

[1] For discussion of solo as continuo, see F. Blume's preface to his edition of K. 537 in Eulenburg's pocket scores, and his essay in the *Mozart Jahrbuch*, 1924.

music of permanent worth—the composer's delight in creation. I do not think that the new rondo he wrote for it when he first settled in Vienna (K. 382) shows that quality in so marked a degree as does the original finale, but the student can judge for himself now the 'new' rondo has been recorded.

Mozart's letters make it clear that when he first lived in Vienna he felt the pulse of his public. Upon the fact that the D major Concerto, like the Vienna Rondo, was written to please the taste of Mozart's time and place, we must centre our study of the Salzburg works, since they become musically interesting only in so far as the man is evident behind his period dress. The ambitious young man liked a concerto which 'went magnifique'; the sincere artist was bound, sooner or later, to satisfy deeper demands than those of ambition. Moreover, though it was exciting to be a popular success in Milan or Vienna, it was depressing to come home and write music which was merely acceptable, day after day, by the standards of Salzburg and its court. There was a difference between being honoured and successfully producing what was expected. Had Mozart been a smaller man, or just a more easily contented man, like J. C. Bach, he might have lived in his home town till offered a Kapellmeistership in a more lucrative place, all the while 'composing to live' like his London friend. Fortunately for us, Mozart was already living to compose.

Colloredo was not to know the size or integrity of Mozart as an artist. The Mozarts, according to the general ideas of that day, were paid to serve music, as were manciple and cook to serve food, sometimes plain, sometimes festive. It was not the best of servants who, instead of showing grateful attachment to his post, asked for leave of absence with plainly ambitious motives. Colloredo was at least no dog in the manger; he granted leave when he was himself away from Salzburg. To say that he was a cultured and intelligent man is not to praise him; the remark simply implies that he was conditioned by his social position and the type of education it gave him. Any blockhead can acquire a culture unless he is a wastrel, and the archbishop was neither blockhead nor wastrel; his arrogance towards social inferiors was neither the attribute of a true aristocrat nor of a person of imagination. Colloredo was proud of his unusually talented musicians, as he would have been of a gardener whom visitors commended. It is unreasonable to blame him for failing to recognize in Wolfgang's talent the first expression of the world's greatest genius, for Wolfgang's father, himself a musician, may not have been aware of it.

Leopold and Colloredo knew merely that Wolfgang, having been toured as a 'prodigy of nature', would now eclipse the Raupachs and Eckhardts, had he not already done so. Nowadays we can be wise

after the event and seek among Mozart's Salzburg concertos those things which foretell greater works.

To appreciate the sentiment of some of the most beautiful of Mozart's Salzburg works we must consider for a moment the boy's mental state after the family had left Italy for the last time, or just after he had made a visit to the Austrian capital and found return doubly irksome. He had a nature as sensitive as Shelley's, though more tolerant of convention, partly because of his training and protection in a home which he loved, partly because of the success he had enjoyed so far in a world which recognized the same conventions as did Papa and Mamma. Yet through the very works Mozart wrote to please the court of Salzburg there occasionally sings a vein of sentiment which is not to be found in the concertos of the London school. Especially is this manifest in slow movements. That to the second Salzburg Concerto, K. 238 in B flat, begins as shown in Ex. 34. The solo entry which follows takes the form of many an aria or violin concerto; it begins as does the orchestral opening, but then moves away from the original tune, which can thus be used as a ritornello to it. It is the spirit rather than the form of a movement like this which seems to reveal the boy's feelings at Salzburg.

Everything we know about young Mozart seems to point to a late puberty, so that at the age of twenty he indulges the introspection of a normal fifth or sixth former; his nostalgia for the Arcady of sensitive pubescents may well have been directed to Italy, not the real garlicky Italy, but the Italy of J. C. Bach and of all musicians and theatrical folk who regarded themselves as strangers and pilgrims from their spiritual homeland, though that country were as uncharted as Poe's Latin Quarter or the Switzerland of musical comedy. Italy was the land of opera and the aria, the music for which Mozart always pined, and we may note that this vein of poetic sentiment—'romance' is too definitely associated with a later spiritual orientation—is chiefly manifested where the texture becomes vocal. We feel it in this or that Kyrie and Agnus to be curiously anticipatory of the countess's songs in *Figaro*; it suffuses 'Tu virginum corona', the second number of the 'Exsultate' motet; above all it pervades the violin concertos of 1775 which sing and sing all the tender sentiments of a boy expressing his first spring dreams. There was always a secret Italy when Salzburg became unbearably stifling.

There are other finger-prints of the greater Mozart, whose texture nearly always quivers;[1] very frequently the Salzburg writing is nervous with inner rhythmic recalcitrance such as |is seen in the B flat Concerto mentioned above. In the same movement of that work Mozart invents new ways of opposing and combining solo with orchestra—*rapports* is the enviable word Girdlestone was able to use by writing his study in French (Ex. 35).

The six Salzburg concertos are as follows:

[1] A happy phrase stolen from Mr. William Glock.

1. K. 175 in D (using trumpets and drums). December 1773.
2. K. 238 in B flat. January 1776.
3. K. 242 in F, for three claviers. February 1776.
4. K. 246 in C. April 1776.
5. K. 271 in E flat. January 1777.
6. K. 365 in E flat, for two claviers. 1779–80.

No. 3 on this list of Salzburg concertos is poor stuff except for its Andante, and there are movements of No. 1 and No. 4 which are

remarkable only because of their composer's age. Mozart lovers have done much harm to their idol by showing too much reverence for his early and less interesting works. There should be frank discrimination between great Mozart and shallow. While it is not my purpose to examine, movement by movement, a fresh and jolly affair like K. 175 in D major, or the 'endearing' K. 238 in B flat (spoilt by its silly Finale), a word must be said, not against the Mozart sentimentalists, but against the growing regiment of anti-sentimentalists; their writings recently tend to revert to those of Parry, who had no use for any other Mozart than the Great Precursor. The word 'endearing' used by Blom in connexion with the B flat Concerto shows that he recognizes, as do so many other musicians, a quality in the best early

Mozart which the mature Mozart never recaptured, even when, as in his last concerto (also in B flat) he employed the same simple language as he did in Salzburg. Many very astute and unsentimental musicians are more deeply moved by the vernal tenderness of, say, the early violin concertos, or such technically simple passages as Ex. 36 from the Sinfonia Concertante for violin and viola, written just before Mozart's escape from Salzburg, than they are by the technical virtuosity and magnificence of the 'Jupiter' Finale. (It is noteworthy that Blom uses no superlatives in his remarks upon the most mature and magnificent of Mozart's first movements, viz. that of the C major Concerto, K. 503.) The anti-sentimentalists are sometimes too fond of looking only at technique; harmony in thirds and sixths and the use of conventional rhythmic formulae may be the means of expressing the extreme of loveliness, and sometimes a very minute analysis will show that technique is not so simple as appears at first sight. I have divided Ex. 36 into little *articula*; notice how cunningly the whole sentence sprouts from the simple *a*, which burgeons into *b*, whose tail is imitated in the oboe phrases, and rounds off the passage when it is repeated yet again before the lovely cadence. That is Salzburg music at its best, with its rhythmic *ondoyance* and irregularity, its inspired euphony and tender sentiment.

Whereas the B flat Concerto was written for Mozart himself, the arid K. 242, with three claviers, was for the Countess Lodron, whose husband had a resident position at the Salzburg court, and for her two daughters, who may have been Mozart's pupils. One of the trio seems to have been no very advanced performer, since one of the parts is so slight as to be unnecessary; hence the alternative arrangement for two claviers in the Breitkopf and Härtel edition. I would suggest a third arrangement without even the second piano, if the concerto were worth any reprinting, but the work is written merely to please; let us not forget that a composer who was not burdened with the demands of supreme genius, Mozart's friend and model, 'London Bach', descended a good deal farther than his disciple to please his audiences. He, too, sometimes concluded a concerto with a *menuet galant*; in a certain D major work he cast it in the form of variations upon a tune which would most obviously 'fetch' a London crowd. I quote the second variation and leave the reader to guess the tune, though we usually sing it in the Key of G (Ex. 37).

The Concerto in C, K. 246, fourth of the Salzburg series, is what we call 'well written'; that means 'let us approve and pass on'—but not too quickly. Its first movement testifies to the stylistic bondage of

Salzburg, though gingered with Mozartian mannerisms. The municipal limits may have brought Mozart some benefit akin to that derived by the intelligent student who is made to write within the limits of text-book counterpoint. He is forced to set rhythmic invention to work, and there is more intricacy of rhythms in the texture of the first movement of K. 246 than is noticed by the casual listener. The slow movement is almost as lovely as 'Tu virginum corona', from 'Exsultate', which it much resembles (Ex. 38).

The finale is a *menuet galant*; if the fashionable form and style could have been vitalized, young Mozart would have vitalized them, but these old-fashioned minuet finales are very unlike the sprightly or impassioned minuets of the later quartets influenced by Haydn. Even in Mozart's hands, the older minuet clanks along under the weight of its conscious ornamentation.

Had a date to be assigned to Mozart's first awareness that he was a grown man, with the heavy privilege of following the light within him and leading others by it, it would surely be the closing months of 1776. At the beginning of 1777 came his first concerto to be recognized as a masterpiece. It is so much better than any previous work in the form that its place is beside the concertos of Mozart's maturity; indeed, it is a finer conception than those which first follow after the composer's migration to Vienna. The marked retrogression observed in the concertos written for Mozart's new audiences of 1782 needs lengthy explanation later on, but K. 271 deserves the detailed study which has been allowed to each of the masterpieces of 1784 and 1786.

CONCERTO IN E FLAT, K. 271.   *Completed by January 1777.*
1. Allegro, 4/4.
2. Andantino, in C minor, 3/4.
3. Presto—Menuetto—Presto, 4/4.

Orchestra: Strings, two oboes, two horns.

Biographical Note

Since nothing from Mozart's pen during the previous nine months, that is during the time between the last concerto and this one, shows any sudden access of stylistic or emotional maturity, the fact that such a phenomenon is present in this E flat Concerto leads one to suppose that the occasion for which it was commissioned was more stimulating to young Mozart than we can easily recognize, unless at some time in our lives we have been through a similar experience. The occasion was but the visit of a lady virtuoso from Paris, one Mlle Jeunehomme, who had high reputation as a performer; she was at least something outside parochial and municipal music, and Mozart sought to shine by writing music which need not confine itself to parochial or municipal demands. Moreover, her esteem would commend him afresh locally and also commend the musical novelties which, but for her, might not be acceptable.

1. *First Movement*

WE must be careful not to see the *structural* abnormalities of this work as advances in Mozart's concerto writing. No artistic advance need accompany the intrusion of the solo instrument into those sections which are proper to the orchestra, viz. prelude, first ritornello, and final ritornello, before the legitimate intrusion of the cadenza. Mozart was too great an artist to play this trick a second and a third time; had he done so, he would have established a line of hybrids, and brought about the disintegration of the one form which he, and he alone, nurtured from childhood to glorious maturity. In his concerto, No. 4 in G, Beethoven renounced his attempts to turn the prelude into a symphonic exposition, the symbol of which, says Tovey, is the writing of a second group of themes *in* the dominant, not just *on* the dominant; but there are several concertos by Mozart with sections of the prelude in or on the dominant, just as there are several which pass from one section to another without conventional full closes. Beethoven, like Mozart, retained the spirit of ritornello technique whatever novelties he introduced.

At the same time, it seems clear that Mozart deliberately set out in this E flat Concerto to do something unusual. He was not by temperament an innovator; his operas are Piccinnian rather than Gluckist, and he would have made a vital dramatic work out of Punch and Judy; the only proof of his pudding would have been the eating. The *castrato* disappears, and the living garlicky baritone becomes more genuinely heroic than the soaring tenors of Olympus (or Valhalla for that matter); the plain man finds his own aspirations and foibles, his sentiment and humour, in the hero whose songs he can sing himself, and in the countess every husband sees the wife he could love less selfishly. Mozart transformed concerto with the same lack of any *declared* plan of campaign, but the novel trespasses of the solo in K. 271 constitute one of his rare experiments. They are quite unlike the glorious and dramatic gambits of Beethoven's G and E flat Concertos, but they are proper to the nature of the one work in which Mozart uses them. For Mozart's solo in this first E flat Concerto is like a young giant eager to run his course. The surprise of the Salzburgers at Ex. 39, the opening of the concerto, was not at anything bizarre, not even at something capricious; the abnormality is artistic, and when, before the orchestra has finished its prelude, the solo is trilling on its long B flat shake, it is preserving its character, as it is when it goes off immediately afterwards and has its own little introductory tune before the band calls it back to the starting-post of a proper exposition. Ex. 42 shows the next abnormal intrusion of the solo, during the first ritornello.

The real advance of Mozart's powers as a concertist is seen in the masterly organization of materials; in this work alone, that organization underlies music which still has the vernal beauty of Salzburg Mozart; the concerto sheds a radiance which makes it to-day more popular than its more mature, more rich brothers in the same key. It has strength, beauty, and youth, and its spirit can best be called athletic. Justification for this description will be recognized, and words will be spared, by study of a structural diagram:

Prelude	A	B	C	D	E	F.
Exposition	x	A	Free		D	y	Free.
First ritornello	E.
Middle section	B	C (lengthily developed).
Recapitulation	A	D	y	B	Free.
Last ritornello	E	A	Cadenza F.

Ex. 41 shows the pair of tunes here labelled by the single letter D; they represent young Mozart's most tender lyricism. But the C which precedes them is the vehicle for the new advance in organization; by it, Mozart links together his texture, altering it and inverting its new extension, as at Ex. 43, to give us the first middle section which can properly be called development. The cross-handed technique and the series of modulations, rapid for those days, provided a novel musical experience for Salzburg. Masterly, too, is the condensation and new sequence of themes in the section which we call by the drab name 'recapitulation' only because its new adventures do not happen to be thematic. The means by which Mozart achieved his condensation, and yet gave no sign that would make the listener aware of the process, can be examined by comparing Ex. 39 with Ex. 40, for the two passages are the transitions A–B and A–D of exposition and recapitulation respectively. The magnificent cadenza is in keeping with the rest of a movement in which every free passage has just the right length and brilliance to be functional; there is no excuse for a modern performer who uses any other cadenzas than those the composer provided for the first and second movements of K. 271.

2. *Second Movement*

Here again the original hearers, who were surely unacquainted with C. P. E. Bach, met something unusual at the outset, for this concerto was probably the first they had known to employ the minor key.[1] A comparison of this C minor piece with the C minor slow movement of the later Salzburg Sinfonia Concertante for violin and viola is forced upon us through the similarity of their opening phrases. Still more noteworthy is their spiritual kinship, since they are for such different performing media. Each work has a sad dignity most adequately expressed in the tone of a solo viola, and it is curious that the opening of the slow movement of K. 271 happens to lie in the alto register.

The orchestra plays a long and expressively articulated melody, coming tragically to a unison forte cadence in C minor. It begins the same theme again while the solo plays a descant, veering away from its original course in the manner of an aria. Thus the first playing of the tune, on the orchestra, becomes an operatic ritornello, and we are reminded no longer of the viola in the Sinfonia Concertante, but of a sad, queenly heroine singing a contralto lament. The modulation into major at the end of the first solo strophe, Ex. 44, maintains the spirit of opera seria, as also does Mozart's expressive cadenza. Like the first movement, this andantino is perfectly, though more gently, held together by simple developments and imitations. It is the first of several movements which are not exactly arias and not exactly binary sonata forms.

3. *Finale*

In studying this movement we must be careful, as in our examination of the first movement, not to lay too much stress upon the abnormalities which arrest attention at our first glance over the score. True, we see a chain of directions—presto, andantino, minuetto, cantabile, adagio, presto—but were there only the presto we should have an excellent *durchkomponirt* finale in rondo form. The piece rattles off with a theme based upon the repeated cadential chords

[1] J. C. Bach wrote at least two concertos in minor keys, but Salzburg could hardly have known them.

found in Monostatos's 'Alles fühlt der Liebe Freuden'; like the rest of the presto materials, it is a little nothing in itself, but it has 'open

ends'. Exx. 45a and 45b show how Mozart can give us A–B, A–C, or B–A, and the whole seems to point to a new type of *perpetuum mobile*. Such a finale has something in common with that of the next E flat Concerto, the wonderful K. 449, which heads the list of truly great concertos from Mozart's pen. The Rondo of K. 449 is made of very different materials, but its incessant cake-walk is brought about by the same 'open ends' method.

The unusual elements in the Finale of K. 271 cannot be regarded as mere mischief *pour épater le Salzbourgeois*: experimental though the inclusion of a slow section within rondo framework may have been, Mozart repeated the practice more than once, and used a minuet for the purpose in his last E flat Concerto, K. 482. We may therefore ask: Why did Mozart continue to make irregularities within the rondo form while never again interfering with the structural principles of a first movement? The answer lies in the fact that rondo, was much looser than the first-movement form which had been imbued with Mozart's ideals of organization; granted those ideals and a composer of Mozart's imagination and craftsmanship, we have twenty-three ground plans to twenty-three first movements. The rondo, on the other hand, has but one structural principle, that of strophic refrain; variety can be obtained by playing about with whole strophes—one can either present the refrain in varied forms, as Mozart does in K. 449 and as others before him had done with less brilliance—or one can insert novel sections between the refrains, as in the concerto we are now discussing. Rondo is present even if refrains come in unexpected places or in unexpected keys: bring a first movement ritornello into the wrong place or with the wrong theme and there is chaos —the chaos not infrequently found in new concertos.

A description of the irregularities in the finale of K. 271 is meaningless without the score; with it, description is unnecessary.

Inquiry has yet revealed neither the occasion nor the two performers for which Mozart wrote his sixth and last Salzburg Piano Concerto. The date of its composition is equally obscure, being sometime between January 1779, when he returned to Salzburg from the tour of Munich, Mannheim, and Paris, where his mother died, and November 1780, when he set off for Munich again. Mozart had composed a great deal since the E flat concerto for single piano; there were the brilliant but not very profound works for Paris and, among the compositions immediately preceding the Two-piano Concerto, the lovely Sinfonia Concertante for violin and viola which takes precedence of all Salzburg Mozart. His growing hatred of his native city, after returning from greater centres of musical activity, is well known and documented from his own letters. His mood during these last Salzburg years may have been aggravated by something else which is not so directly expressed by the young man. He sincerely loved his father. The affection of father and son was due not a little to the fact that Leopold was himself a fine musician; but Wolfgang was more, and Leopold may not at this time have fully understood that more. It speaks much for Wolfgang's devotion to his home that his answers to some of Leopold's letters were not more tart and frank. The man who had passed his twentieth year surely felt that he would be nothing as an artist until he carved his own way of life, independent of home or the opinions of Salzburgers. He must have regarded some of Leopold's advice as that of an over-affectionate parent who is trying to prolong his son's childhood. Yet Wolfgang's answers to passages like the following are evasive, or written with a childish (consciously childish) humour which he hopes will pacify his father, and it is clear that Leopold is sometimes so charmed by the prattling language which seems to say 'I am still but your little boy' that he cannot express his exasperation forcibly enough for it to be effective. The following letter is typical of many:

L. Mozart to Wolfgang, 11 February 1778:

'The purpose of your journey was two-fold—either to get a good permanent appointment, or to go to some big city where large sums of money can be earned. Both plans were designed to assist your parents and to help your dear sister, but above all to build up your own name and reputation in the world . . . it now depends on you alone to raise yourself gradually to a position of eminence, such as no musician has ever obtained . . . it depends on your good sense and your way of life whether you die as an ordinary musician or as some famous capellmeister of whom posterity will read—whether, captured by some woman, you die bedded on straw in an attic full of starving children or whether, after a Christian life spent in contentment, honour and renown, you leave the world with your family well provided for and your name respected by all.'

What use had a mind of Mozart's size for 'a famous capellmeistership' or for the belief that a good Christian will be rewarded on earth by success among men? Allowing for the fact that Mozart had been brought up with ideals of respectability and safeness—ideals formed by the cruel need to maintain possession and increase it if possible—one supposes that the wording of some of his letters may have been a deliberate affectation to appease the father whom he loved. We do not find expressions of horror at the secularity of other musicians, nor assurances that religious observances have been made, in letters to other people than Leopold, but the Mozarts wrote little to persons outside the family circle.

Leopold seems as bewildered as the mother of the ugly duckling when his son is in a temperamental mood quite normal to artists:

'Your remarks—I am tolerably well—I often wonder whether life is worth living—I am neither hot nor cold—I don't find much pleasure in anything—seem to indicate that you were discontented at the time of writing or were in a bad humour. I don't like it but I can't say anything about it.'

More disturbing than Mozart's subjection to his parents, at an age far beyond that at which most men have launched out for themselves, is the possibility that some of his observations may be sincere. Just how should one regard the following? 'That godless arch-rascal Voltaire has pegged out like a dog, like a beast! That is his reward!' And when we inquire just what Voltaire's reward was, and why his death was beastly, we find that Wolfgang's pretended or sincere horror—I wish we could think it pretended—is due to the fact that Voltaire refused the last rites of the church! Had the greatest natural genius in the world a mind of that dimension in things that did not directly affect music?

Allowing for the moral and social conventions of Mozart's time, one still cannot understand why Wolfgang was held in his father's protection and native city as late as his twenty-fourth year. Let those who find it hard not to succumb to Mozart-worship (so tremendous is the appeal of his best work, so enchanting the finish of his second best) make deliberate notes upon everything about the man which it is difficult to explain. Where was his reading, his interest in anything other than music and drama? When throughout his life did he make an attempt to 'improve' himself as did Beethoven? Were dancing, billiards, and boredom his only occupations when not engaged musically? Why did he marry at all unless he could find something more worthy of his genius than Constanze? (Or is that too hard upon Constanze? Perhaps she was a greater woman than we know.) Was it fear, the basest of all emotions in an artist, which made him shun philosophy and remain in the safety of unquestioned orthodoxy? I posed these questions to a man who is not only more deeply versed in Mozart's chamber music than any other musician I know, but whose love of Mozart would never lead him to evade a frank answer. Without his permission, I make the following quotation from his answering letter:

'I believe it to be almost literally true that to Mozart life was music and nothing else, and that explains the points you mention. He wanted to marry so as to have the things done for him that only a woman can do, as well as to keep quiet the sexual side of his nature, as he says quite frankly in a letter to his father. A woman with any personality of her own would not have filled the bill. He could write a charming letter to her, but he may not have cared very much for her in his heart of hearts. He needed someone passive and that is what he got. I don't believe there was room in his head for thought about religion or philosophy. After all, he did not live to the age at which Beethoven began to be Beethoven, and the years of his maturity were crowded enough in all conscience. His father had turned him out a specialist with a specialist's limitations, and one cannot but notice in his early letters from Italy how little notice he took of anything outside the sphere of music—it was the price he paid for being what he was.'

It is not the purpose of this book to give another life of Mozart, nor even to feel his mental pulse at various stages of his life. All we are concerned with at the present moment is that, at a time when Mozart's dissatisfaction in Salzburg was reaching its climax, we have the Two-piano concerto which is permeated throughout with a kind of staid happiness. I shall not give it the full examination allowed K. 271, since the employment of two keyboards causes alterations which exclude the concerto from a rightful place in the series.

1. The orchestra has little to do outside its prelude and two main ritornelli, the one in dominant and the other in tonic.
2. The interplay of band and keyboard, which makes such notable advance in K. 271, finds counterpart here in the interplay of two pianos.
3. The slow movement is not a long C minor aria as in other concertos by Mozart which happen to be in E flat, but a tissue of short melodic materials and their embroideries, all in a still-smiling major key.
4. There is hardly any place in Mozart's scheme for the kind of writing proper to a solo performer. There are no free *bravura* passages.

Yet the work is an enjoyable one which has proved a favourite at promenade concerts; this is probably due to its smiling euphony and the wealth of short, pretty tunes (Exx. 46 and 47). Recordings are available, but I should not call people insensitive who heard the records during meals; recently, while using Mozart as food-music, one was forced into an abrupt caesura in mastication during the Finale of K. 365 (Ex. 48).

Lengthy baroque counterpoint having been unacceptable in

Mozart's day, there is no point in the remark that Bach's part-writing makes better two-clavier concertos than K. 365. With the later materials the wonder is that Mozart's duetting is so good; only his

ingenuity could have devised continual cross-rhythms consistent with homophonic taste. It is said that players get more pleasure from the performance of this work than do listeners, and one can believe it by imagining oneself in the skin of one of the players. The fingers have their own memory.

In the concerto, as in the Two-piano sonata, the first player sometimes finds himself a sort of continuo-man to the other, sometimes

giving him a piece of imitative repartee, sometimes pressing out the
tune, at other times embroidering it for his partner, and sometimes
finding the greatest pleasure of all in filling up the other man's rests
with neat little exclamations, ornaments, and trills. Though first
intended for Mozart and his sister, Nannerl, the double concerto,
with added clarinets, trumpets, and drums, was often played subse-
quently in Vienna with Josephine von Aurnhammer, whose performance Mozart admired greatly. She pestered him for lessons, and
is said to have been enamoured of him.

Before again leaving Salzburg in November 1780, in order to prepare *Idomeneo*, which had been commissioned for Munich, Mozart
wrote one very lovely work, as well as church music and the 'Thamos'
incidental music for Schikaneder's theatre. The work referred to
is the glorious three-movement Symphony in C, K. 338, honour-
ably known as 'Beecham's favourite'. Its first movement combines
Mozartian wit with a majesty that calls for Schubert's C major trombones; its last movement is one of his most vivid finales, and its slow
one of his loveliest, second to none of its kind, if it has any kind; to
describe its haunting sinuosity one must steal the phrase 'heavenly
length' from Schumann. After the Munich production of *Idomeneo*
came the Oboe Quartet, then a return to Salzburg—the last time as
servant. On 12 March 1781 Mozart left for Vienna, where Colloredo was already staying. What happened there is well known. Had
Mozart been differently brought up, to think and fight for himself,
had he been less his fond parents' Mass-goer and Penance-doer,
relations with Episcopal Highness would have been settled years
previously and in a more dignified manner. Neither Colloredo's
behaviour nor that of Our Hero, as judged by his own correspondence,
did either of the pair credit during the time immediately preceding
Count Arco's notorious kick.

Trouble with the archbishop being over (though Mozart's letters
show that he feared Colloredo even after dismissal, and did not want
to go back to Salzburg where the archbishop might arrest him or 'get
at' him) there followed trouble with Leopold, who disapproved of the
engagement to Constanze. We gentlemen's gentlemen are gentlemen,
and what sort of people were the Webers? We read Leopold's homi-
lies on respectability; in some, he points out to his son the difference
between Wolfgang's parents who, by keeping themselves to themselves, got and held a position which the neighbours respected, and
Leopold's vagabond brother whom, apparently, the Salzburg Mozarts

did not visit in open day. Wolfgang is a chip off the old block sometimes, as when he speaks of a performer on the fiddle, whose fee
included a suit of clothes, 'a beggarly request'. Our modern snob-
beries take different forms, and we must not blame Leopold for his
opinion of Constanze.

The first Vienna concertos do not appear from Mozart's pen till
late in 1782, at least a year and a half after his arrival in the capital.
The end of 1781 was occupied with the composition of *Die Entfüh-*
rung, but early in 1782 we read of his playing in the Augarten. He
had plenty of concertos already composed which would be unfamiliar
in Vienna, and a 'great favourite' with his new public was his first
Salzburg concerto—K. 175 in D. The new year is an important one
in the history of concerto form, for in 1782 Mozart began his career
as player and composer; by 1784 he was recognized as the leading
concert performer of his day.

CHAPTER VI

1782. EARLY VIENNA CONCERTOS

THE CONCERTOS OF 1782. *Written during the autumn of that year*

1. *Concerto in F major, K. 413.*
   (a) Allegro, 3/4.
   (b) Larghetto, C, in B flat.
   (c) Tempo di menuetto (Rondo), 3/4.
Orchestra: Strings, two oboes, two horns. Two bassoons are added for the second movement.

2. *Concerto in A major, K. 414.*
   (a) Allegro, 4/4.
   (b) Andante, 3/4, in D major.
   (c) Allegretto, 2/4 (Rondo).
Orchestra: Strings, two oboes, two horns.

3. *Concerto in C major, K. 415.*
   (a) Allegro, 4/4.
   (b) Andante, 3/4, in F.
   (c) Allegro—Adagio—Allegro, 6/8 : 2/4.
Orchestra: Strings, two oboes, two bassoons, two horns, two trumpets, two timpani.

THE following remarks summarize the most important developments to be observed in the 1782 concertos:

1. The first of the three concertos, K. 413 in F major, despite the advance in workmanship, shows a retrogression in *style* from the last Salzburg works, particularly K. 271 in E flat. We must seek some explanation.

2. The three concertos are progressively novel. The second, in A major, is popular because of its gaiety and happy themes which have been described as 'among Mozart's most Tyrolese'. The third concerto, in C, makes daring new departures of structure as well as the more obvious additions to the orchestra. The texture shows a new contrapuntal interest, and modern ears suspect no continuo-work in the solo part.

3. The group is orchestrated both more carefully and more personally than was any Salzburg concerto. In particular, the viola seems no longer to have the last-written line of harmony, as a mere double to the bass, or as a third participant between bass and fiddles.

4. There is a marked advance in the keyboard writing. The student will gain much by examining Mozart's piano sonatas of the period. The cadenza to the C major Concerto is among Mozart's finest.

5. The first movement of each of the three concertos represents a type which recurs among the fourteen concertos of Mozart's Viennese maturity. Each type is marked by a distinctive orchestral prelude. Thus:

(a) The first type, exemplified by the F major, is of a homogeneous nature, seen in most of the Salzburg concertos and inherited from J. C. Bach. The subjects are not outstanding, being neither forceful, nor dramatic, nor of a prolonged lyrical nature. Yet Mozart often reverted to this homogeneous type of first movement and did so for his very last concerto. Workmanship consists in the organization of a mass of small materials, as exemplified in the first movements of K. 451 in D, K. 453 in G, K. 456 in B flat, and K. 537, the 'Coronation' Concerto in D.

(b) The next type I call the melodic, represented by the second concerto of 1782, the A major. Here we meet good tunes which vibrate in the memory because they are fewer in number than in 'homogeneous' concertos. Melodic concertos begin with a tune and not a gesture. Their orchestral preludes may make polyphonic busy-ness out of a specially introduced gesture, but they are more concerned with the chief tunes, which the solo faithfully repeats or translates into its own keyboard language. In this respect the A major Concerto of 1782 is little brother to the other A major, K. 488, and should soon be no less popular now that recordings are available.

(c) The last concerto of 1782, the C major, is of an altogether more ambitious type. Its opening is contrapuntal and uses brass and drums, together with as much wood-wind as Mozart was sure of obtaining at the time. Notable successors in the same manner are the concertos in the same key, K. 467 and 503, to which, despite the great disparity of workmanship, K. 415 has remarkable similarity of conception. The second and third movements are formally more satisfactory than the first, the final Rondo being one of Mozart's most attractive.

CONCERTO IN F MAJOR, K. 413

In discussing separately each concerto after this 1782 group, which represents the final stage of Mozart's apprenticeship in the form, analysis is preceded by brief biographical notes which the informed reader may like to skip. Descriptions of purely musical procedures, so inept without reference to the score, and hopelessly attempting to translate into words the untranslatable language of music, are difficult to omit when one wishes to mention processes developing within a composer's musical imagination. At present, for instance, we are faced with the question: 'Why, after the stimulating E flat Concerto, K. 271, and the concerto in the same key for two pianos, is there a retrogression in the first concerto of the following year? Why does the F major Concerto of 1782 hark back to the older, *galant*, undramatic style of Mozart's boyhood, though there is no retrogression in artistry?'

The answer is that Mozart was no longer playing or composing for a known audience, trained to accept the development of a highly personal self-expression. (Contemporary evidence[1] shows that Mozart's work was thought to be both novel and disturbing at times.) For the first time since he was toured with his parents, Mozart faced an audience whose taste and indulgence had to be measured. This is no matter of inference; several letters to his father discuss the fact. Let it be remembered that it was Mozart and not Beethoven who first dared to live upon his talents without the intermediary protection of a patron. Many a contemporary as well as his father must have thought him a presumptuous young fool who would come to heel after his first taste of freedom and poverty; both he and his father were Micawbers, thinking that something would turn up, but each had his own idea of the nature of that something. Leopold looked for a Kapellmeistership in the capital, which would give the Archbishop food for thought; Wolfgang wanted Vienna to recognize him for what he was—the artist who, in opera and concert, expressed the finest aspirations of his fellow-creatures. Had he lived longer, he might have found a patron, by which term one means a patron-admirer of the Beethovenian epoch and not a patron-employer of the old régime. Or perhaps a circle of patron-friends would have grown among aristocratic well-wishers and brother freemasons; or Mozart might have made direct contact with the people, as he did with *The Magic Flute* in Schikaneder's theatre, and so have anticipated the romantic

[1] Even the autobiography of Dittersdorf, Mozart's friend and admirer.

triumphs of Weber. As it was, he was free—free to thrive or starve with his new wife in old Vienna, where printer or copyist could make more money from new music than its composer could, and where newly composed music could bring immediate money only by performance or by subscription printing. So we must again ask: 'For whom were the concertos of 1782 written: what sort of people had Mozart to please if he were to make a living?'

These concertos were written for patrons of the subscription concerts which Mozart himself gave, and for 'academies' like those held on Sunday mornings at Baron van Swieten's. We know that from his youth onwards Mozart's heart was fixed upon the writing of opera, so that while he was engaged upon his first full-scale *Singspiel*, *Die Entführung aus dem Serail*, other works, such as sonatas for friends and pupils, concertos for audiences either at subscription concerts or in the Augarten, were almost by-products, however much inspired. Mozart's main sources of income were not, as they would be to-day, performances which the immediate popularity of *Die Entführung* gained for that work in various Austrian theatres. There is no evidence that Mozart received any money after his fees for the first performance. The young people depended largely upon well-to-do pupils and the proceeds of concerts attended by the same pupils, their social equals, and other members of the musical public.

It is significant that the first work composed for the city whose musical pulse Mozart had not yet felt was the Variation-rondo in D for piano and orchestra, a mere series of variations and coda upon a jejune and well-ornamented theme. Sets of variations which were not intended for a place in one of the greater concertos show little more than grace and facility. A lightly constructed rondo was expected after the first two movements of a concerto, just as a minuet was expected to relieve what the public regarded as tension after the more intricate or serious opening movements of a symphony. Mozart obeyed only his own artistic conscience when a finale showed any higher organization than was customary.

Can there be any doubt concerning Mozart's reasons for substituting the Rondo-variations in D, K. 382, for the Finale in sonata form, when he played his D major Concerto of 1773 (K. 175) at his first concert before the Vienna audience in March 1782?

That concerto is of the old homogeneous type, and when the first 1782 concerto followed, in the autumn, it reverted to the same style. Its last movement is a rondo of the older Italian plan; its main theme a courtly minuet. There is little in the first movement which sounds to our ears like inspired utterance, though it is one of Mozart's rare first movements in 3/4 tempo, a measure which usually brings the agitated, even passionate, expression which we find in K. 449 or the great C minor Concerto; with this time-signature we expect Mozart to put sforzandi on weak accents, to syncopate, and use cross-rhythms between members of the orchestral ensemble, or between band and soloist. Those who look at the movement with no special eye to main themes, but with a backward glance at the older Salzburg concertos to whose style it seems to turn, will find that its texture is not quite so conservative as is its general mood or character—if it can be said to have a character of its own. The first solo entry is, as usual, made into a pleasing novelty (Ex. 49).

There is nothing retrogressive in the scoring; dynamic contrast, staccato pointing recalcitrant to the solo and auxiliary to it, cross-rhythm within the orchestral parts—these are as plain as in the best Salzburg pieces. The viola, for instance, has a part worthy of a good musician and is even required to use double stopping. Yet in no place do the wind instruments play independently of the strings, nor is their writing 'exposed'; and despite keyboard passages in more than two parts, and other passages in which the hands cross, the whole of the solo part could be played as a sonata, for the left hand always gives the bass. In other words, the player still retains something of the function of clavier-ripienist. A very fine cadenza to the movement is published in facsimile by Mandyczewski.

For all its tameness, the slow movement charms. It uses the Alberti bass throughout, but we know from movements like the middle one of the popular F major Sonata (K. 332) how beautifully Mozart can employ the device.

The last movement is ingenious. The form demands that an old-fashioned minuet tune, which must have been written with conscious amusement, shall be repeated three times. Mozart keeps to the courtly measure throughout the movement, but the tune is more than a mere refrain, and its re-presentation is more than the varying of figuration (triplet bass or redistribution between band and solo) to be found in a set of variations like the D major Rondo to the revived K. 175. The original minuet has the A, A, B, A shape of many a traditional song or dance, and consists of four phrases of eight bars; but each eight-bar phrase can be further articulated into two four-bar phrases, so that Mozart can make little jig-saw rearrangements of the components which provide the required modulation here, refrain effect there, or transition to or from episode in another place.

Algebraically; AB.AC.D.AE can turn out later as AB.AX.E.AD or as any other reshuffle of material; yet so perfect is the sleight of hand that we are never conscious of manipulation. As a result, this rondo is very much more satisfying than many of those movements in rondo form which illustrate the mature workmanship of Mozart. Without this ingenuity, the steady minuet time and the closed cadences would become tedious.

One is tempted to quote a good deal from this movement, showing how Mozart gave the public what he thought it would like, while entertaining himself with workmanship not inferior to that of previous concertos. The scoring of the theme itself at its second return is attractive, though to the unmusical listener it evokes pictures of the French ball-room, with a fellow bringing down a big ceremonial stick like the drum-major's on each first-of-the-bar (Ex. 50). The coda, with final diminuendo, is beautiful.

CONCERTO IN A MAJOR, K. 414

This work is as satisfying as most of the later concertos, and should one day share the popularity of K. 488 and of the clarinet quintet in the same key. It could be called the artistic equal of K. 488 but for the wonderful slow movement of that later work. In K. 414, which retains throughout its course the sunny mood which we associate with Mozart's compositions in A major, we are not brought into contact with the introspective Mozart, and the consequent consistency of the work is our compensation. It was just such a work that Mozart needed with which to charm the public on whom he had been careful not to experiment. Beneath the Tyrolese charm of this second concerto of 1782 there is a considerable technical advance.

The whole spirit of the concerto is set by its tuneful opening, which is of the kind to be repeated by the solo entry. Thus the work is less novel from a structural point of view than its predecessor in F major.

With lengthy and well-marked first and second themes, Mozart seeks new stuff for his middle section, the piano heading off, just as in the A major Concerto, K. 488. Certain materials remain purely ritornellic and the solo has neither part nor lot when they recur. The two principal subjects, of which an Austrian audience could hardly fail to be enamoured, show such keyboard translations as are seen in the cross-hands technique of Ex. 51.

One more quotation, Ex. 52, will serve to show the similarity between much of the figuration here and that of the later A major

Concerto, and also an insistence upon ornamental discord which, though seeming unworthy of mention, happens to be a Mozartian characteristic not markedly prevalent in the household vocabulary

49.

50.

51.

of Viennese keyboard music before Mozart. Noteworthy too is the close similarity between parts of this concerto, notably the swinging second subject, and corresponding parts of the little A major Symphony of 1774, K. 201.

Though in D major, the slow movement is serious, untinged with melancholy except in the portions which modulate to a minor key. The modulations are made by a haunting extended cadence (Ex. 53)

typical of Mozart's later writing. The orchestra opens with an organ-
like theme sixteen bars long, the whole strophe coming to a troubled

rest with the cadential figure, so simple and lovely, which Mozart
uses in the modulatory paragraphs (Ex. 54). This movement, so
different from the previous slow movement with its continuous
Alberti bass, is worthy of a place among the greater concerto movements of Mozart's maturity. Before leaving it, we may quote the

introduction to the cadenza, wherein Mozart still dwells with affection upon his cadential figure, keeping the full harmonization which is characteristic of the movement.

A cadenza, not a mere scale-plus-shake, should be played. The concerto was a favourite with the composer himself, who wrote two cadenzas for each movement, though the first set seems the better. All the cadenzas show plainly how long such pieces should be. Their function is to prolong material with the soloist's meditation or display, but not to set up a use of that material which shall rival its former treatment in length or intricacy. For the slow movement, Mozart's cadenzas are not a dozen bars long; for the first movement, despite the greater speed, they are not twice that length. When will pianists either use Mozart's practice for a model or, still better, play Mozart's cadenzas where they are available? How much better than the obtrusion of an academic exercise from Leipzig or Paris!

There is nothing imposing enough in the rondo to be put in an album, but the movement is a good one. Let it not be condemned for its frivolity. The apparent heartlessness of such movements is not acceptable to people of some natures. Occasionally—very occasionally—Mozart wrote witty music without any obverse of sentiment, and it is difficult for us to acknowledge the fact when we meet it. Our comedy is larded with sentiment, which finds its way alike into our native ballad opera and into our variety entertainment, which must perforce include moral verses or the Song at Which No Gentleman Laughs, be its subject patriotism, flowers, animals, or merely unappeased appetites and defective hormones. *The School for Scandal* ends with its affecting homily on marital fidelity. There is an unwritten catalogue of subjects which are not entertaining, and Great Music is not entertaining. More respect will be paid to a new symphony that is feeble but serious than to a new work which is feeble and trivial. The scowl on the surface is taken for an assurance that the composer does not intend to waste our time, though the sobersides wastes more by the clock than does the playboy. Medicine should taste nasty if it is doing good. I have heard a brilliant musician ask why Beecham lavishes as much care upon a 'silly' Rossini overture as upon a tone-poem by Sibelius, though the Sibelius piece is comparable with the overture as to inspiration and originality.

Let it be admitted that there are few Mozartian concerto rondos which are merely entertaining and clever, which never show a temporary obverse of sentiment. Plain fun is not typical of Mozart, and those movements in which there is no moodiness, no bitter-sweet, no sigh for the transience of passing loveliness, are rarely great examples of technical virtuosity. Yet when an admirable movement does show unchecked high spirits, we must put aside our Saxon solemnity and recognize worth. What a difference between this jolly Rondo to K. 414 and the D major Rondo, K. 382, written to replace the Sonata-finale to the D major Concerto! It is also a finer piece than the alternative Rondo-finale to the A major Concerto, also written at this time.

The second A major Rondo, K. 386, is a well-formed work despite its inferiority to the movement which it replaced. The manuscript was sold by auction in London in 1840. It was torn into separate sheets, of which all but two out of ten or eleven have disappeared. Fortunately Cipriani Potter made an arrangement for two pianos which he published in 1839, and which was rediscovered a few years ago by C. B. Oldman. On the basis of this and of the manuscript fragment, Dr. Alfred Einstein has made his edition of a composition well representative of the *Seraglio* period.

Manipulation of form does not itself make a rondo fire or misfire, but in the K. 414 Concerto rondo there is an interesting departure from convention. It is usual for the refrain to be heard just after the middle section has concluded, but in the A major Concerto it is held back to be played by the soloist just after the cadenza.

CONCERTO IN C MAJOR, K. 415

For so prolific a man, and for a composer who died so early, Mozart left behind a proportion of second-rate work which his worst enemies could not call disgraceful. His magnificent integrity as an artist has not been duly recognized as a virtue; it has been regarded as heaven-sent. We are inclined to applaud skill, in games as in art, which shows no apparent effort. The 'effortless', the 'inborn artistry and impeccable taste', are thought to be part of Mozart's genius, reinforced by the standards of an age which had more taste than feeling. Even concertos like this not very successful one of 1782 show that every time he expanded his materials Mozart's perfection was brought about by mental effort. He acknowledged the fact concerning the quartets dedicated to Haydn, and we should note that the new contrapuntal developments and more powerful cast of themes found in those quartets are very like the strides not quite successfully maintained in this C major Concerto. For all its faults, the concerto should be played occasionally to show its ambitious conception.

The first movement textures so absorb his interest that he makes the parts greater than the whole. The parts can be seen at a glance in those passages quoted (Exx. 55–7). A fine middle section, Ex. 58, lies on the same page as writing for the keyboard which might come from a sonatina. The inequalities of the prelude are typical of the movement; beginning with Ex. 55, it proceeds to the customary forte passage, thence to the beautiful 'close' writing, Ex. 57, which reminds

55.

56.

us of the Sinfonia Concertante or the 'Haydn' Quartets. So far, so good; but none of this material is used by the solo.

The forte passage, Ex. 56, is made the gambit of one of Mozart's finest cadenzas. In the Steingräber edition, one H. Schwarz provides his own cadenza in the main text, and informs us that Mozart's will be found in the appendix; but what we find, when we turn to the appendix, is Mozart arranged, puffed, and made palatable by H. Schwarz. The impudence does not consist in cooking Mozart's cadenza, for we do not know how it was served by Mozart himself, but in (a) giving H. Schwarz pride of place, and (b) insulting the player's musicianship by attempting to foist Schwarz upon him as genuine Mozart.

The rest of the movement is filled with abortive improvising that Mozart himself parodied in 'Ein Musikalischer Spass', and of which Ex. 59 will serve as a specimen. The intrinsic poverty would not matter were the writing functional. The first two bars of Ex. 55 merely pop up here and there; yet I believe that if Mozart had looked at the score of K. 415 at the time when he was writing K. 503 in the same key he might have made a fine thing of the earlier

57.

58.

59.

movement, retaining the prelude intact. The first new solo tune of the earlier concerto is brother to the later one (see Ex. 60).

After the slow movement, which merits no long examination, comes one of Mozart's most engaging variants upon the rondo stereotype, A, B, A, C, A, B, A. The most apparent novelty is the use or an adagio paragraph in C minor, together with a change from 6/8 to 2/4 tempo, making the section called B. But greater ingenuity lies in the invention of a refrain with three tunes, of which Exx. 61 and 62 are the first and third. When this refrain, with its triple form *a–b–c*, has been announced and followed by the C minor adagio passage, it never recurs in the same form; we get *a* each time, but it may be followed by a middle tune other than *b*, a different third tune than *c*; or it may have one of its tunes developed to a greater length than in the original *a–b–c*. A notable use of this procedure is found right in the middle of the movement, which Mozart fills with a farrago of the rondo tunes and solo *bravura*. The usual strongly distinguished

middle section with a change of key, making a movement of its own, would have been inartistic where the minor-key adagio is already so distinctive.

A musical friend who shares my liking for this rondo once helped me to recognize the great difference between the works of 1782 and those of Mozart's artistic maturity, two years afterwards. I had expressed the wish that the K. 415 Rondo might sometimes be played after two movements of one of the later C major Concertos, since I thought it musically superior to their proper finales. My friend answered in words rather like the following: 'I think the incongruity would be evident; fine though the K. 415 Rondo seems, you are thinking of it in terms of 1782. A single work of an earlier period may be a more perfect realization of its ideal than one of a later, more rich, period; but the difference of conception would show if there were any lopping and grafting. In the case you suppose, the scoring alone would show.' That is true; the added instruments of K. 415 do not make for any greater interplay of solo and orchestra. The chief participants in concertante sections are strings and piano; we are far from the kind of concerto which Spohr, in a famous gibe, called a duet for wind and piano. Reflection on the talk with my friend led me to wonder what we should have thought of Mozart's concertos had they ceased after 1782; Mozart would have seemed little more than a J. C. Bach with a turn for eccentricity in structural matters, and with a fine ability to write good tunes of the kind demanded by the taste of the day.

How great is the difference between the concertos of 1782 and those of 1784 which begin Mozart's mature series! The works bridging the gulf between them are remarkably few in number for so prolific an artist, but they are of a new and very high quality. Chief among them must be mentioned the first three of the six quartets dedicated to Haydn. The first, in G major, was finished by the last day of 1782; its chief interest lies in the contrapuntal mastery of its finale, and the marked advance in the treatment of its thematic material. Another work, the splendour of which should gain it a more frequent hearing, is the C minor Mass which was to have been for Mozart's nuptials; he took it with him to Salzburg in 1783, when the young couple visited Leopold and other Salzburgers such as Michael Haydn. Despite its incomplete state, its magnificent counterpoint and its choral effects bear comparison with Bach's B minor Mass in more than one item. Yet no examination of all these works can fully explain the vast difference between the first concerto of 1784 (K. 449 in E flat) and any previous work in the form; artists reach their stylistic maturity each at a different time of life, and that maturity is sometimes shown in one type of work before another. Thought, industry, reflection on matters outside music, such as the nature of society (Mozart was becoming interested in Freemasonry at this time), the study of other men's music, including that of older masters—all these things may be prompted by an inner natural growth, and, in turn, may influence and accelerate that growth; but the growth itself remains as much a mystery as the opening of a flower; it would seem to be outside the artist's power to control and certainly outside the critic's power to explain.

CHAPTER VII

CONCERTO IN E FLAT, K. 449

CONCERTO IN E FLAT, K. 449. *Completed by 9 February 1784*
  1. Allegro vivace, 3/4.
  2. Andantino, B flat, 2/4.
  3. Allegro ma non troppo, 4/4.

Orchestra: Strings, two oboes, two horns *ad libitum*.

Biographical notes

Mozart and his newly married wife were found at various addresses, and he had become the favourite piano player in the capital. The years 1784–6 must have been among his happiest; he enjoyed acceptance as a virtuoso, the new married life, the success of *The Seraglio*, in Vienna and many other cities, the stimulation of the six quartets he was dedicating to Haydn, and the interest of the older contrapuntal music, particularly of Bach and Handel, which was favoured at Baron van Swieten's Sunday 'academies'. His wife urged him to write fugues. He gave private concerts. He held a ball in one of his lodgings, and we may read a list of names of the lions who graced it. He hoped for success in the world; he charged the highest fees for lessons and determined not to lower his pride either by accepting from any patron a permanent post which was not adequately paid, or by hinting to influential friends that he would welcome this or that employment. If he accepted any official position, it would be on condition that time and opportunity was provided for travelling and free-lancing.

In the year 1784 Mozart wrote no less than six concertos for the piano. Of the group of three, in E flat, B flat, and D (K. 449–51), which begin the mature series, the first was written for Babette or Barbara Ployer, Mozart's pupil for clavier and composition; her father, Court Councillor Ployer, was agent for the Salzburg court in Vienna. Although all three concertos were written between 9 February and 22 March, there was another ready for Babette by 12 April—the magnificent Concerto in G major, K. 453. Mozart's composition exercises for her are preserved in the Vienna National Library; she must have been a very gifted pupil, for we hear no complaints such as Mozart sent home concerning his ladies in Paris, one of whom could not add to a simple minuet. Extracts from letters about the group of three concertos are as follows:

1. *To Leopold Mozart. 20 February 1784.* 'The concerto [the E flat] you may have copied. Remember, do not show it to a single soul, for I composed it for Fräulein Ployer, who paid me handsomely . . . how can I protect myself from the engraver, who can surely print off as many copies as he likes and therefore swindle me? The only way to prevent this would be to keep a sharp eye on him. Yet that was impossible in your own case, when you had your book [the violin tutor] printed, for you were in Salzburg and the printer was at Augsburg. I almost feel inclined not to sell any more to an engraver but to have my compositions printed or engraved by subscription at my own expense as most people do, and in this way make profits.' Mozart's next letter shows a list of subscribers for the engraving of some compositions, possibly earlier concertos or sonatas.

2. 'The first concert on Mar. 17th went very well. The hall was full to overflowing and the new concerto I played [Babette's E flat?] won extraordinary applause. Everywhere I go I hear praises of that concert.'

3. *To Leopold Mozart in Salzburg. 15 May 1784.* 'I gave to-day to the mail coach the symphony I composed for old Count Thun in Linz and also four concertos [the three with K. 453 added] . . . I do ask you to have the four concertos copied at home, for the Salzburg copyists are as little to be trusted as the Viennese . . . and as no one but myself possesses these new concertos in B flat and D, and no one but myself and Fräulein Ployer those in E flat and G, the only way in which they could fall into other hands is by that sort of cheating. I myself have everything copied in my room and in my presence. . . . The E flat Concerto can be performed à quattro [with strings only] without wind instruments. . . .' The next letter, in which Mozart speaks of the B flat and D Concertos, written for himself, as 'concertos that make one perspire', is well known. He is again anxious that nobody shall get hold of copies . . . 'only to-day I could have got twenty-four ducats for one of them, but I think that it will be more profitable to keep them by me for a few years more and then have them engraved and published'.

4. *To Leopold Mozart. 9–12 June 1784.* 'Please tell my sister that there is no adagio in any of these concertos—only andantes.' In view of the maltreatment of so many slow movements which Mozart does not mark adagio, this letter is significant for modern players.

HAD I to mention the three or four Mozart concertos whose neglect was most unjustified, I should head my list with K. 449, the first of Mozart's mature series. The great C major, K. 503, admired by Busoni and by Tovey, might claim priority for the grandeur of its first movement; the little B flat, K. 456, should have a place if only for the poignant slow movement, one of the few slow movements in variation form to which the adjective can be applied; but the E flat work to be discussed now has three unique movements, each worthy of its two fellows, and this cannot be said of the four or five concertos which already obtain favour in our concert halls. K. 449 is altogether a great work. A soloist can distinguish himself more by expressive discipline than by pianistic virtuosity, and this platitude of concerto criticism applies very specially to a work which needs a mind capable of directing the concerted numbers of *Figaro* rather than two superbly trained hands which can rap through every published volume of Liszt.

1. *First Movement, Allegretto Vivace*

Were this movement shown to a body of musicians who were not aware of its origin, and were they allowed to see no more of it than the first three or four themes of the orchestral prelude, nobody could call them fools for surmising that here was the orchestral accompaniment to one of the great concerted scenes from Mozart's operas. So unusual and so important is the operatic influence that most of the preludial themes are quoted (Exx. 63–6). They seem to belong to a dramatic altercation. The first one changes mood after a mere four bars; after another eight the tremolo bows are storming in the minor key; thence we find ourselves listening to music which expresses the changing thoughts and exclamations of a character moved by rival or conflicting impulses, or by the presence of other personalities on the stage. In Ex. 65 do we not hear Susanna and the Countess bickering, then pleading, in first staccato thirds then flowing sixths? Who can resist singing ' Susann', or via sortite! Sortite, così vo' ?' after the imperious thumps of Ex. 67? And though the lovely transition passage over the dominant pedal in Ex. 66 recalls the Sinfonia Concertante for violin and viola, it occurs time after time in operatic scenes.

This operatic music, described by Girdlestone as having an *inquiétude fiévreuse*, would give the soloist no other work than to join in or to put the mood phases into relief by the plainest, but most clear and purposeful, figurations. The piano writing in this movement has therefore appealed only to the soloist who is musician first, who loves the work as a whole, and delights in being *primus inter pares*. In more than one place the piano seems the only means of pouring oil upon troubled waters, yet in few concertos is the solo

more essential or more worthy of a soloist who is more than a performing animal.

With the abnormal antithesis of moods we note the abnormal con-

63.

64.

65.

66.

67.

densation of structure. Judged by the watch, the movement is as
brief as it is crowded, though its fullness deceives us, as does each of
its fellow movements and for the same reason. A bar's cadential
shake ends the first exposition for the solo, but there is no similar

phenomenon at the point where, in a normal concerto, the first ritornello ends and one of the partners, usually the piano, heads off the
middle section. Indeed there is no clearly defined first ritornello and
middle section. As soon as the piano has done its shake in the dominant key, the band makes its Almaviva gesture (Ex. 67), and after
seven bars the piano is again arguing; the dispute settles down into
the opposing of two invertible themes, and we are right in the middle
section whether we know it or not. The quarrel lasts not half a
minute before a chromatic climb by the piano brings us to the
reprise. Mozart's cadenza for Babette Ployer is also exceptionally
short and brusque, in keeping with the rest of the movement, and he
must be a charlatan who plays any other.

Of this movement and concerto, rather than of certain later works,
can it be said, as the older text-books said of Beethoven's first concerto, that 'it sets the orchestra free'; but it does a good deal more
than this; it sets Mozart free as a concerto composer. There are
several Mozarts, and not everybody admires them all; but who is not
fascinated by that greatest of Mozarts, the creator of Figaro, Elvira,
Papageno, Basilio, and the Countess? In the E flat Concerto we are
now discussing, this Mozart first dares to show himself in an instrumental work, and though the expression of human emotions during
the period of the supreme operas cannot but have fertilized the
instrumental writing in all his later symphonies and concertos, in
none of them is the operatic influence so direct as in this E flat
Concerto.

2. Second Movement, Andantino

To continue the operatic feeling of the opening movement would
be ineffective; one expects, and gets, relief from its tension in a movement of extreme tenderness which, though in the major key (B flat)
and by no means complex or disturbing in itself, is strangely like the
calm after tears have been shed. Its material consists of two strophes
of lengthy cantilena by the orchestra, repeated or decorated by the
piano in a way so advanced as to bring us into Schumann's piano
kingdom. Mozart here is what Joseph Surface called 'a man of sentiment', and does he not enjoy the game! It is the kind of writing in
which he deliberately indulges in the unprepared seventh for cadences
on the dominant chord, and in melody with romantic descending
minor sevenths such as we find in Schumann, or in Elgar's 'Enigma'
tune. I do not suggest that Mozart is at all insincere, only that, like
Gilbert's wandering minstrel, he knows what he is about.

Though this movement is not in sonata form, it is certainly *durch-komponiert*, each of its strophes developing. Despite Mozart's later fondness for the Romanza with its simplicity and full closes, I find

much greater pleasure in these slow movements of more substantial construction, even when the building is as slight and effortless as in the present instance. Elsewhere I have spoken in defence of the Romanza with its repeating refrain, though the repeats tend to make Teazles of us all in the presence of 'a man of sentiment'.

How remarkably different are Mozart's slow movements *when a piano is present* from those of his symphonies and quartets! Is it his reflection that the keyboard succeeds the harp and lute, with their amorous associations, that imparts to Mozart's andantes a distinctive tenderness in the best sonatas and concertos?

3. *Third Movement, Allegro ma non troppo*

The Finale is the crowning glory of this concerto. It is one of those brilliant conceptions which can be brought forth once, but never imitated.

Superficial analysis cannot but call this movement a Rondo, just as it cannot but call the 'Jupiter' Finale a Sonata-form. Any good student can write a fugue wherein obedience to rules of stretto will ensure climax, just as the rules of entry will ensure cohesion; but even a brilliant student like Mozart failed sometimes to write a good rondo, and where the failures occur concertos may go up like the rocket and come down like the stick. To vitalize rondo, Mozart had several methods; one was the introduction of contrapuntal mock-solemnities; another the playing of ducks and drakes with entries of the refrain, or the adding of extra tunes where the refrain was previously expected; another, that used here, was the ingenious altering, extending, redistributing, and otherwise gerundially treating the refrain itself. Beethoven was a master at that game, but in this E flat finale we have a quite un-Beethovenian version of it.

The refrain is the be-all and end-all of this rondo. If the little tune (see violin part in Ex. 68) is not marching upon stilts across the stage, it is lurking in the wings while its episodes mark time, ready to give us our second, third, and fourth smile when it reappears in a different hat (Exx. 68–70). The episodes are *petits riens* whose function is simply to maintain marcato movement, and but for the final entry of their leader in 6/8 dress the whole piece would be a *moto perpetuo*. A piece of one of the episodes, Ex. 71, using cross-hands, once more reminds us of *Figaro*. The bass is a prediction of Almaviva's petulance in the recognition sextet of Act 3. *Al fiero tormento* growls the Count; *Al dolce contento* purr Figaro's happy parents.

The four re-dressings of the refrain could not have been made by a composer who was not an adept in academic counterpoint; any student can force contrapuntal imitation, but it is *style*, even in the modification of a single part, that tells the contrapuntist. One could easily force the theory that the entries of this refrain were intended to bring a laugh against the series of text-book 'species' which seem to be parodied in turn. The ease of these variations would have been impossible to the Mozart of a few years before this time. This is not the place in which to discuss Mozart as a deliberate contrapuntist or to estimate his stature as such in comparison with other composers. But he and Haydn alone among contemporaries brought off a fusion of homophonic basis with contrapuntal ornament or stiffening, without the strenuousness that there is when even Beethoven's sonata movements put on lengthy contrapuntal attire. So sure is Mozart's sense of contrapuntal style that in all kinds of unexpected places—the final presto of *Don Giovanni*, for instance—he makes a *fugato* gesture which leads us to think that we are going to have something on the scale of the 'Jupiter' Finale; yet when the parts disappear in smoke, or find themselves on firm homophonic ground, we are aware of no incongruity. So in the Finale to this concerto, one or two feints at a fugal head-off serve, as do the episodic pieces, only to impart a wonderful uniformity of movement. The whole piece seems without divisions; that is why it is unique among concerto rondos. The only movement I can recollect which makes an interesting parallel is the finale to Haydn's 'Drum-roll' Symphony, despite its very different texture and tempo. A study of the two pieces shows more vividly than all the writing in the world the difference between two turns of genius.

There may be greater concertos than K. 449 in the offing, but none more consistently inspired or more perenially interesting.

CHAPTER VIII

CONCERTO IN B FLAT, K. 450

CONCERTO IN B FLAT, K. 450. *Completed by 15 March 1784*

1. Allegro, 4/4.
2. Andante (E flat), 3/8.
3. Allegro, 6/8.

Orchestra: Strings, two oboes, two bassoons, two horns. One flute added
in the last movement only.

Biographical notes

The second of the group of three, K. 449–51, was written less than
five weeks after its predecessor, so the work needs no extra biographical notes. Mozart's letter explaining that the wind parts were
essential to its performance, whereas K. 449 could be played with
strings alone, should not lead us to suppose that it is the more interesting work orchestrally; the strings in the E flat work are used as
never before in a concerto—far more passionately and colourfully
than in this work, which is essentially for the keyboard virtuoso, for
Mozart himself and not Fräulein von Ployer.

There are few greater surprises in the chronological order of
Mozart's concertos than the following of K. 449 in E flat by K. 450
in B flat, a key favoured by Mozart more in his keyboard works than
in his symphonies, and nearly always a medium for wit and juxtaposed
sweetness. Mozart was aware of the unusual contrast. In a letter to
his father of 24 May 1784, he writes:

'I cannot come to a decision between those two concertos in B flat and
D. I consider them both to be concertos which make one sweat; but the
B flat one beats the one in D for difficulty. Moreover I am anxious to
know which one of the three concertos in B flat, D and G you and my
sister like most; for the one in E flat is not at all in the same class, being
a concerto of quite a peculiar kind' [my italics].

Mozart then speaks of the smaller orchestra for the E flat, but I
hope our examination of that work has shown that size of band does
not affect freedom or range of instrumental writing. If the E flat

emancipates the orchestra, the B flat gives the pianist his fling and, in doing so, harks back in many ways to the earlier non-operatic Mozart. Indeed a lengthy passage in the ritornello (Ex. 73) comes straight from one of the Sonatas for organ and orchestra of Salzburg days, whether Mozart was conscious of the fact or not. It well illustrates a point made elsewhere concerning the promise in Mozart's immature work. Every eighteenth-century concerto has a figure based harmonically on the common chord followed by the dominant chord, with or without the seventh, and a melodic line whose main accents come on the component notes of those two chords . . . the very opening of this particular concerto is no more than this (Ex. 72). With young Mozart there is very often a rhythmic crispness or sententiousness, simple enough when once heard, but rarely appearing in parodies of Mozart, and not appearing in a similar way among Mozart's great contemporaries nor in early Beethoven, whose originality comes not from the novelty of his themes but from the breadth of his style and his unconventionalities; those who look for Mozart's greatest invention only in the great temperamental or abnormal works, in *Don Giovanni* or in the 'daemonic' concertos, must find it difficult to understand one's delight in such works as K. 450, of which there are more in number and quality than there are concertos of the calibre of K. 466 in D minor and K. 491 in C minor. I can but assure the reader that, though subtlety may hide behind what looks at first like stock-in-trade Mozart, I shall not hesitate to declare when I feel that invention is lacking.

1. *First Movement, Allegro*

FROM the very outset, and for reasons given above, this concerto reverts to an older style than the operatic K. 449. Its first tune might belong to a serenade for the Haffners' neighbours, or, as it first appears on oboes and bassoons, with octave-horns-honking-in-upon-accents, it might have been written for a steam merry-go-round. Yet even here is the stamp of genius. Tovey has pointed out the witty change of accent at its half-way mark. The stuff that follows is deliciously and quite unusually scored. It has an amused urbanity perhaps not pleasing to those who carry the apostolic succession from C. P. E. Bach through Haydn and Beethoven; for here is the music of J. C. Bach lifted by subtlety and genius into virtuosity. This is the *galant* style deliberately and affectionately adopted by an

artist who had spoken with the expressiveness of the previous concerto. The only operatic convention, used both in the prelude and
again later, to make the cadenza enter at a climax, is the 'conspiratorial' crescendo over a pedal-bass.

The band has two functions in this movement, (*a*) to support and
provide ritornelli for the most virtuosic of Mozart's solo parts, and
(*b*) to make gnomic decoration. So slight is the accompaniment, so
few the places of interplay, that at first examination of the score one
would suppose that the band need be present only for ritornelli. One
would be mistaken, owing to the fact that the piano writing gives a
new freedom to the left hand; it no longer completes the bass for the
right hand at all places.

Tradition has it that this is the most difficult of concertos for the
soloist, and one may safely say that, if the previous concerto emancipates the orchestra, this one chains it again. Once the prelude is over
we have nothing less than a piano cadenza which revels in one key
and recalls Bach's organ toccatas. The flourish concludes with a
pirouette and a pause *sur les pointes* on its last two B flats, before
stepping off on its whimsical path (Ex. 74). So full of *bravura* is that
path that no material from the prelude punctuates the solo performance until the first main ritornello.

There is no parallel phenomenon in any Mozart concerto, nor is
there any parallel to the ensuing middle section, which only the deaf
would call a development. Nothing is developed but the pianist's
technique. So far as 'emancipation of the orchestra' goes, we might
be at the stage of Bach's fifth 'Brandenburg' Concerto. The middle
section of this K. 450 shows no theme thrown from key to key between band and solo as a ball between clever players, no opposition
of cunningly antithetical motives specially prepared or derived. All
is virtuosity for the piano; and Mozart has his reasons.

For the recapitulation is the triumph of this movement. One point
in which Beethoven vastly improved upon his predecessors was in his
unwillingness to repeat tamely at the end of a sonata-form the exact
order of the subjects in his exposition, with tonic instead of dominant
or relative major harmony. The diagrams in my chapter upon the
structure of Mozart's concertos showed that Mozart was aware of the
dullness of repetition only when a form, such as concerto, threatened
to present material three times in the course of a movement—in
the orchestral prelude, in the concertante exposition, and in the
reprise section. To avoid such dullness Mozart rarely allowed the
exposition to repeat more than a small portion of the prelude, but

when there was fuller repetition (as in the popular A major, K. 488)
he prepared an abnormal treatment in the sections that followed.
Usually, as we saw in the diagrams, he introduced new second
themes in the solo exposition, which might be used for the middle

section or in the cadenza, but did not appear in the recapitulation. It is not quite accurate to assert, as someone has done, that Mozart's recapitulations always followed the order of material in the prelude, though it may be taken as a rule that material shunned in exposition and middle section appears, as in this movement, during the reprise. What happens in this masterly recapitulation is a synthesis of almost every theme in orchestral prelude and solo exposition, so that the section tamely labelled 'recapitulation' is climactic to the whole movement, with its apogee at the cadenza. The *bravura* nature of the work, so far from causing weak construction, gives opportunity for a constructive *tour de force*, not immediately obvious either to haters of the *galant* style or to its uncritical lovers. A diagram may be useful; two points in it are worth noting; first, the difference in the two ritornelli, and secondly the substitution of a new theme, z for x, at the final parade of themes.

Ritornello material	A B C D E.
Exposition	Cadenza A x *Bravura* y *Bravura*.
First ritornello	B E.
Middle section	Accompanied *Bravura*.

Recapitulation	A B z *Bravura* y *Bravura* C *Bravura*.
Final ritornello	D Cadenza D E.

2. *Second Movement, Andante*

There is little in this movement which can be enlightened by verbal description; its procedure as much as its spirit is entirely self-communicating. A point may therefore be discussed here concerning all Mozartian slow movements, after we have briefly noticed the plan of this piece.

The movement consists of two variations and short coda to a theme in flowing 3/8 time, the whole being in E flat; but the theme is in two strophes, modulating in the middle to the dominant key; each strophe is repeated in each variation, making a kind of double variation.

The tune begins with conjunct movement, unlike the slow movement of K. 449; it is much more placid, and is not of the kind chosen for surprises in variation. Mozart's wisdom is seen in his making a halt after three full treatments, so that we wish there were more, despite the rich degree of satisfaction we have experienced. It is a platitude of musicography that variation-tunes are of two orders, those chosen for their simple and definite character, so that the variations can take great liberties and astound the listener by their adventurous transformations, and those which are so lovely that they will bear repetition with different instrumental clothing, and will spoil if radically altered. The conjurer-and-pumpkin treatment given to the first type is shown by Beethoven in the 'Diabelli' Variations

and by Brahms in his Handel or Haydn sets; the 'vibrates-in-the-memory' treatment belongs chiefly to English composers, and is seen in Byrd's sets for virginals, Purcell's harpsichord lessons, Dowland's 'Lachrymae', and Delius's *Brigg Fair*. This slow movement is one of the few instances of Mozart's use of the English Way in variations. The piano embroideries are elaborate and difficult, but the melody remains unaltered even in its 3/8 time-signature. It has none of the repeated notes of the tunes used for the brilliant variations in concerto finales, as in the G major and C minor Concertos, K. 453 and

491, nor does it use sequences. That a comparison with Delius's methods in *Brigg Fair* is not altogether ridiculous may be seen by the extract given at Ex. 75.

Girdlestone notes that the theme puts us in mind of the organ voluntary played before a church service. One cannot think that Mozart meant to evoke a religious atmosphere, though we need not despise his taste if such was his intention. Church musicians are prone to think that the fashions of their own age show better taste than those of any other since Elizabethan and Palestrinian times. At the present time anything modal, or pseudo-modal, anything which observes speech rhythm, is superior in taste to music which shows only clear style and breadth of conception. Not all chromatics are sugary and fit only for the theatre, or Bach's harmonizations of chorales would be expelled from the choir. This slow movement has been turned into an anthem which is in the repertory of several anglican cathedrals. Performed in a sloppy way it seems just what Hollywood seeks to help the jilted bride bedew the Madonna's feet with glycerine. Such a movement must be played in a carefully decided tempo, without any rubato, with clear phrasing and control of tone. Sentimental or didactic performances are an affront, for they imply that the performer knows more about the work than composer or audience.

3. *Third Movement, Allegro, 6/8*

The sun does not go down upon any Mozart Concerto in B flat. Much has been written upon Mozart's reactions to keys, notably A major, E flat major, D major, C minor, G minor, and D minor, but discussion leads to no conclusions except that works written in a certain key have similar moods. B flat is one of the happy keys and this is one of the happiest of rondos. It is full of pianistic tricks (Ex. 76), one of which, with its hand-crossings, reminds us of the Rondo to Beethoven's C major Concerto. The particular phrase, Ex. 78, is such a commonplace that no importance need be attached to the similarity.

Tovey has pointed out Schumann's solemn transformation, in his Piano Quartet, of Mozart's impish refrain (see bass of Ex. 77), but Tovey does not admit that Mozart's Rondo is less well put together than the Schumann movement. (To Tovey Mozart was one of the classics, and to see weakness in a classic and to mention it was considered by him to be 'perky'. The danger with smaller brains than

Tovey's is that, by adopting his attitude, they will make themselves feel every mistake with an august signature to be a unique piece of humour or whimsy.) In this Rondo, despite its splendid keyboard writing and its engaging materials, there are one or two extraordinarily weak transitions. Would one accept Ex. 78 from an advanced composition student? Only a prig would call this puckish humour, and he would call it nothing of the sort if it came from a concerto by Muggs instead of by Mozart.

One does not defend; one merely seeks an explanation of weakness from the pen of a highly self-critical artist. Where Mozart saw a constructive task, as in the making of a first movement for a concerto, he surmounted it. As he approached Rondo, he saw that it needed enrichment and fertilization, and enrichment and fertilization he gave it in several notable instances which we have studied before coming to this Finale. But Mozart may not have considered that Rondo needed closer knitting. Beethoven, whose themes are designed for large-scale architecture, would not and did not accept rondo as a parade of loosely strung tunes. Mozart added to the tunes, altered their order, varied the refrain, introduced dramatic episodes, and in general added to the spirit, the wit, or the versatility of emotions in Rondo; but he seemed to accept its structure as a slight matter, with perfunctory transitions as part of its character. At this stage of his development the B flat rondo satisfied him.

One who is not a trained pianist and whose hands cannot stretch beyond the octave find this finale even more difficult than the first movement. The very light action and slightly smaller dimensions of the keyboard in Mozart's day must have put less tension upon the muscles and made the virtuosity just a little easier to attain, but the mere snippets quoted here in music-type will serve to show that K. 450 Concerto remains primarily virtuosic to the end.

CHAPTER IX

CONCERTO IN D, K. 451

CONCERTO IN D, K. 451. *Completed by 22 March 1784*
1. Allegro assai, 4/4.
2. Andante (in G major), 4/4.
3. Allegro di molto, 2/4.

Orchestra: Strings, one flute, two oboes, two bassoons, two horns, two trumpets, two drums.

Biographical notes: as for K. 449 in E flat.

THERE are signs that make one hope for honoured places in concert programmes for many a neglected Mozart concerto. One can hardly hope for performances of this D major Concerto except in a series of concerts which follows the complete list of mature concertos, including this specimen along with its two predecessors of March–April 1784.

A keen Mozartian who has never set out upon a special study of the concertos at least knows a dozen of the best, but it is doubtful if he knows K. 451 even though he knows of it. I did not even possess a score of it before I began to write these notes. I had never been attracted by the snippet printed on Breitkopf's covers for purposes of identification. Yet of the three movements, only the finale is trivial. My first duty, then, is to explain why I was not enthusiastic about a work of which its composer thought highly.

Mozart's contemporaries found his music as often disturbing and novel as they found it complaisant; except in works like serenades, cassations, dances, and divertimenti, during the performance of which there were, no doubt, other activities than listening, we can hardly accuse Mozart of pandering to the taste of his time. This concerto seems to represent only its period; yet when Mozart was conservative, he was sincerely and intentionally conservative.

Many of us begin with an admiration for Mozart like Schumann's admiration of the 'Hellenic grace' of the symphony. We taste the period flavour and then discover the great personality behind the period technique, as we think it to be. But, living even nowadays in the sunset of the great romantic epoch, we judge all lengthy works by their emotional appeal and by the individual stamp of their chief themes. We tend to like Mozart's works in minor keys or in a magnificent style like that of the last symphony, applying almost a moral test, as Matthew Arnold did when he said Pope's writing lacked 'poetry and high seriousness'. Not everyone who unconsciously sides with Arnold is a school inspector, or a sobersides who thinks that spiritual turgidity or magniloquence are the inevitable concomitants of greatness. We may or may not be right in our values, or in our looking for character in leading themes; the point is debatable. We can be certain, however, that such an attitude prejudices us against many works by Mozart of which he thought as highly as he did of this concerto. The letter to his father quoted in connexion with the three concertos, K. 449-51, proves the fact.

Mozart may write at his best where there is 'poetry and high seriousness' or, as in the D minor Quartet and the G minor Quintet, where he expresses a dejection too deep for tears; but, once familiar with the materials of these introspective works, we suppose that their themes are more highly individual than those of more undisturbed and undisturbing compositions. It is obvious that Mozart's themes grew more apt to his purpose as he progressed as a concertist and artist generally. The shaping of them to his ends may be seen by studying, side by side, the openings of his first and his last Concertos in B flat, K. 238 and K. 595, as at Ex. 79. But is the theme of that last concerto any *more highly individual* than the theme of the sunny little Salzburg work? Often, as in both these themes, a synthesis of material is made from units which are not in themselves prepossessing. The academic first and second subject of many a Mozart sonata is not really, as so often called, a beautiful melody, but a synthesis of *articula* which will lend themselves both to metabolism in development and to 'open end' jig-saw fitting. It is only the total result which measures Mozart's genius; take away that genius in the concertos and we have only the talent of J. C. Bach, the music of an age.

To acknowledge that the total result can bear the imprint of genius when the details seem common, one might remember two other Concertos in D major as well as this K. 451—let us say the Haydn concerto and the 'Coronation' Concerto. Neither is a work of first rank, but if one is more typical of its age than are the others, which is that one? Why is each different in general character and effect from the other two? The answer may come during our special study of K. 451.

1. *First Movement, Allegro assai*

That very mastery of transition, that polishing and planing, that easy balance which we sometimes regard as typical of the eighteenth century, is actually personal to Mozart, through whom chiefly we know the music of his age. In this orchestral prelude we find Mozartian homogeneity at its finest in concerto form as far as we have followed that form.

The presence of a flute with the usual oboes, horns, and bassoons, the new delight in sforzandi, and the contrast of dynamic strengths, all make a texture which would as well introduce a symphony as a concerto; its elements are the small change of music—the brass tantara-raras on 'open' notes, the Salzburg ♩♪♪ rhythm for fiddles on the first beat of the bar, the iambic downward scale, the crescendo over a pedal bass in repeated quavers. Which of these elements will be used in this or that particular place once the movement is in full career?

If we were to judge only by workmanship, there could be no finer first movement in the series; its character lies in its total effect. The only parts which will interest many a listener are not in the main structure but in transitions such as that from first ritornello to middle section. After the customary shake by the solo at the end of its exposition, the orchestra enters with a downward iambic scale, but this ritornello does not reach its close, for the piano chimes in with a happy imitative point that dovetails ritornello into middle section. Even in this concerto Mozart has his novelty (Ex. 80).

Not only does the movement flatter text-book talk of a double exposition, but it *sounds* symphonic. One would suppose it to have been written to show the abnormality of the previous concerto, the B flat, which has a very marked personality, an extremely virtuosic solo part, and a prevailing mood of caprice. But in the D major all is synthesis and interplay; the sections pass through all the material of the prelude, yet never does the piano translate a single ritornellic

theme into keyboard figuration. The 'new' expository solo tunes (the
x and y when we use a diagram) are definite though no more memorable than other themes in this very homogeneous piece. In no con-

certo does the solo speak more clearly both through and with its newly
augmented orchestra, and the movement can be ruined by a pianist
who is not master of the rudiments of his art, who cannot play scales
and arpeggios with perfect firmness of touch and time. So often
these elementary accomplishments are lacking in performers who
attempt what they consider much more ambitious work.

Its texture can be as easily spoilt by a conductor with poor sense
of structure; yet how many conductors, even of high repute, can keep
perfect periodicity for more than thirty bars, or gauge the exact control
of a crescendo? With a Mozart in charge, this movement might not
seem dull; it is certainly not shallow for all its facility, and though it
is nobody's favourite it took no less concentration in its making than
did its more attractive fellows in the other 1784 concertos.

2. Second Movement, Andante

It is better to risk making an ass of oneself by writing 'I do not
like' this movement, than to indulge for the sake of style in presumptuous Johnsonisms like 'the interest retires'. For many, the interest
grows directly a concerto reaches any movement called Romanza.
The present writer does not share that interest, being among those
who like slow movements of stronger construction.

Mozart himself showed as much affection for these strophic
andantes as for such magnificent sonata forms as the slow movement
in the G major Concerto which follows this one, or for those slow
movements such as that in the well-known A major Concerto, whose
artistry makes the return of their principal subject a pleasure rather
than a necessity. It is not the simplicity of a Romanza that one finds
a little wearying, for what a wealth of simplicity is to be found in *The
Magic Flute*. One does not tire of the Andante in the 'Little Night-
Music', which happens to be simpler in outlay than this Andante of
K. 451, and whose chief tune is very like it in one place (see Ex. 81).
The ground plan is that of a small Italian rondo, and, though this is
not the structure of Mozartian Romanza in its final form, we have
here the adumbration, particularly as regards character, of the type
which became Mozart's favourite form of Andante in piano concertos.

It is the character of these Romanzas which one finds tiring. Their
languor has no parallel in Haydn or any other composer; the word
and the movement are apparently Mozart's own.[1] They may belong
to some idealized Italy, but they recall Batt's imaginative cartoon of
Mozart looking listlessly at a billiard table. (The drawing may be
unjust and unrepresentative of the lone Mozart.)

It is admitted that the composer used the utmost of his melodic
powers upon andantes of this Romanza type; they have no parallel

[1] Mozart does not actually call the Andante of K. 451 a Romanza, but it plainly
is of the type called Romanza in later concertos.

in any single song from one of his operas, for no character seems ever
to be placed in a situation which calls for the expression of so passive
an emotion.

3. *Third Movement, Allegro di molto*

Little more is to be found in this Rondo than aptly turned themes
taking their apt turn-and-turn-about. The solo writing is deft enough,
but the themes are not worthy of a concerto so imposingly launched
as this one. We need not spend long with a rondo which sees fit to
make sequences like Ex. 82. Even the final appearance of the refrain
in 3/8 time is a lamely used example of Mozartian practice. The only
point worth noticing in the whole movement is that the Rondo is
opened by the orchestra and not, as usual, by the solo instrument.

CHAPTER X

CONCERTO IN G, K. 453

CONCERTO IN G, K. 453. *Completed by 12 April 1784*
  1. Allegro, 4/4.
  2. Andante (C major), 3/4.
  3. Allegretto—Presto, 4/4 (Variations).
Orchestra: Strings, one flute, two oboes, two bassoons, two horns.

Biographical notes

1. *Letter to his father, 9 June 1784.* 'To-morrow Herr Ployer, the agent, is giving a concert in the country at Döbling, where Fräulein Babette is playing her new concerto in G, and I am performing the quintet [K. 452]; we are then playing together the grand sonata for two claviers [K. 448]. I am fetching Paisiello in my carriage, as I want him to hear both my pupil and my compositions.'

2. *The next letter, 21 July.* 'When you have tried over the three grand concertos, I should be glad to hear which you like best.' Mozart is here referring not to the 'Group of three' (K. 449–51), but to the first three of 1784 which had essential wind parts, viz. K. 450 in B flat, K. 451 in D, and the new G major. It is difficult to know why the middle one of these three should be esteemed as highly as the others. Leopold liked the key D major, and, as the public of Vienna still held K. 175, with its new rondo, as a favourite, we see what difference time makes in taste. (Actually this second letter is addressed to Mozart's sister, but the father would, of course, see it. He wrote frequently to Mozart at this period telling of the progress Nannerl was making as a clavier player.)

THE second of Mozart's concertos for Barbara Ployer is one of those few concertos in the series wherein each of three movements reaches a supreme level of excellence; pejorative criticism is not always unfair when it declares that a slow movement, or a finale, is unworthy of its fellow movements in the same concerto. In one or two examples one cannot explain this fact only by the taste of Mozart's audiences or by the necessity to write lightly after preceding movements. Mozart was quite able to write three fine movements, each fine *by its own stan-dards*, even when this included tunes as shallow as street songs. In this G major work Mozart set that standard from which he was not again to fall, though he never wrote a better concerto of its kind. There are three glorious movements as there were in the previous concerto for Barbara Ployer, K. 449.

1. *First Movement, Allegro*

The very outset of the G major Concerto shows its peculiar charac-ter; it is complex, even magnificent. Its slow movement is profound —one of the three greatest of slow movements; yet the concerto is intimate. For all its horns and the added flute it can say all it has to say in a much smaller room than a concert hall, and even in that place makes one feel that one is among a circle of performers, not in an audience. It will be noticed that its opening march tune is played softly and, after the still more 'softening' F natural, takes on a far from martial sequence; it is made all the more intimate by the wood-wind flutters (Ex. 85). Three qualities of this movement may be studied here:

1. The influence of Mozartian comic opera.
2. The confirmation of certain structural principles.
3. The careful keyboard writing for Babette Ployer.

To each of these, then, a paragraph of comment, which claims to be no more than personal; any value that lies in the comment will come from the reader's reflection and not from his assent.

In our examination of K. 449 in E flat, the former Babette Ployer concerto, we saw how, despite its small orchestra (wind parts being, as Mozart told his father, unessential to performance) the scoring for the strings was exceptionally moody and rich in effects, such as sfor-zandi and tremolo bowing, as if inspired as much by imaginary characters on a stage as by the apposite development of a concerto. We are not to know if concerto form would have taken the path it did under Mozart, or if it would have moved straight to its later nineteenth-century form, had its greatest exponent been other than an operatic composer. Certain it is, however, that the conventions of concerto, even before Mozart set out to enrich it so wonderfully, were flattering to a master of stage-music; we need only think of one such convention—that if the prelude opens softly, as in the G major work we are considering, sooner or later this initial texture must be terminated by a sudden loud strophe with a good *coup d'archet* on the

first of the bar. (What Tovey has called the 'conspiratorial crescendo'
over a tonic or dominant pedal is another element we associate with
the theatre.) When Mozart developed the form on a scale which
made the prelude into A, B, C, D, E, F, instead of A, B or perhaps

A, B, C, when the introduction of new material for the solo, often
two or three full new themes, demanded the addition of new ritornello themes, then more than ever had the concerto-writer to be an
expert in the expression of constant change of situation and opposition of moods, rather than a composer who dominated a whole
movement with the growth of one theme and mood, as did Beethoven.
I am well aware that no such *problem* presented itself to Mozart, since
he worked from the dictates of his musical instincts; the outcome
may have given him much thought, but its character was as inevitable
as the shape of a nest to the bird that makes it. Ex. 85 then, might

easily have been the introductory music to Figaro's measuring in Act 1; it is in the same key and has the same sly 'knowingness'. Incidental music like Exx. 83 and 84 may belong as much to *Don Giovanni* as to *Figaro*, yet it does not prevent a Mozartian Concerto prelude from remaining a procession of themes.

86.

87.

In the first movement of the first concerto of 1784, K. 449 in E flat, we found the influence of operatic moods; in this G major work we find what seem like operatic situations. The quotations at Exx. 83 and 84 might depict respectively the arrival of a person or a clue, and the suspicious pause before a new discovery changes the action.

It is worth while to make a diagram of this movement, for the principles of ritornello and of 'open ends' are very astutely employed.

Notice C–D and C–x, which dispose of the text-book meaning of recapitulation.

Prelude	A	B	C	D	E F.
Exposition	A	B . . . x . . . D. . . .			
First ritornello	B	F.			
Middle section	E	Y	&c.		
Recapitulation	A	B	C	x	D . . . . .
Final ritornello	E	Cadenza	F.		

(Dotted lines represent free writing.) The middle section uses new material. In Mozart's sonata forms, as exemplified in solo as well as concerted works, the middle section made from previous themes is by no means an ideal; it is but one of many ways of using the space between exposition and recapitulation. The label E is justified at the beginning of the middle section, as will be seen from the flute and bassoon parts of Ex. 86. (The original E theme is the operatic touch seen in Ex. 83 above.) Two other points should be noted in support of this labelling:

1. The theme is brought in with the same dramatic modulation as at first in the orchestral prelude.
2. The customary shake at the end of the first main ritornello is elided for the purpose.

The modulations that follow in this middle section are very personal. Beethoven can make momentous modulations on account of their dramatic placing, especially in recapitulatory sections of sonata forms; Mozart likes modulations for their own sake; they are part of his creative virtuosity, and are therefore in the middle sections of works, whereas Beethoven sets himself to grapple with themes in a way which belies the word 'section' altogether. Ex. 87 shows modulations of a type not heard in concertos before Mozart; they still sound as fresh to us as they did to the first audience.

A letter already quoted tells how Mozart wished his pupils to shine when Paisiello arrived, strange though we may think it that a Mozart should commend his work to a Paisiello! The making of new departures in concertos not written for Mozart himself may be ungenerously thought to show that Mozart wanted to try public taste without risking his reputation as a performer. There seems to be some ground for this remark when we remember the new paths taken by K. 271 in E flat, written for Mlle Jeunehomme's visit to Salzburg, the K. 449 Concerto in E flat for Barbara Ployer, this G major for the same lady, and the B flat work with the G minor Variations for

Theresa Paradies. Yet, if there are any concertos in which, after practice, the average amateur pianist can hope to show his capabilities, they are precisely these works, together with the popular A major, which may also have been written for a pupil. In the G major Concerto we are discussing, for instance, there is only one really difficult passage—the second variation of the Finale, which calls for good left-hand work, and in this Barbara may have been well coached. It does not need a prejudiced generosity to admit that Mozart served his lady performers well. These particular concertos seem, indeed, to need the very qualities to be found in the feminine pianist—provided she can keep strict time, a matter in which the ladies seem greater offenders than their husbands. A glance at the free passages and the very fine cadenzas to this concerto will show opportunities for the display of apparent brilliance, all founded upon the natural positions of the hand which has been trained upon time-honoured methods and has not yet been asked to perform the acrobatic feats of, say, the B flat Concerto (K. 450)—feats which involve the blazing of new trails among the nerves connecting hand and brain. Pianism in this work in G major can be made to sound no less virtuosic than passages from concertos written for the composer himself, but they are the very stuff on which we still bring up good pupils.

2. *Second Movement, Andante*

The opening theme of this movement (Ex. 88) of which I quote the keyboard version, shows it to be one of the most profoundly emotional in the whole series, and also to have the same type of inspiration as a solo aria—but not, I think, an operatic one. An aria-like movement with a very different turn of emotion is the F sharp minor one in the middle of K. 488, the A major Concerto; but whereas that tragic lament comes straight from the opera house, this movement surely comes from the church. Its opening may be compared with that of the aria 'Et incarnatus est' in the C minor Mass (Ex. 89).

This Mass was to have been performed at Mozart's own nuptials, and readers are referred to a biography for the explanation of its postponement. Ultimately, though incomplete, it was performed in St. Peter's, Salzburg, on 25 August 1783, Constanze singing the soprano arias, including the one quoted. It is possible, therefore, that the aria was written less than a year before the concerto. The point is not an important one, but it is surely not fantastic to declare that Mozart could have made a fine Agnus Dei out of the slow movement to the G major Concerto.

The structural technique of the aria is evident from a diagram:

Orchestra	A	B	C.
Solo	A	D.	
Orchestra (ritornello)	C.		
Solo	B.		
Orchestra (ritornello)	A.		

This is followed by entirely new material in G minor, quoted in Ex. 90a and showing, as does the rest of the solo part, those vocal technics, e.g. the virtuosic skip of an octave and a fifth, which were customary at the time. Then all in the diagram above is recapitulated,

so that the whole movement is (mistakenly) said to be in short ternary
sonata form. But there is a notable alteration in the recapitulation,
which makes one prefer the term 'extended aria form', if there must
be such labels. The alteration is the substitution of a new and wonderful strophe, which I will call X, for D. Ex. 90 shows the passages
compared—A, D and A, X. The persistently ritornellic C casts its
chromatic languor over each solo strophe (Ex. 91), and the modulations which lead to the point of recapitulation show a lovely, tortuous
attempt to climb out of depression into the original major key (Ex. 92).

92.

93.

The cadenza is of great beauty—I refer to the first of the cadenzas.
Mozart wrote two to this movement, as to the preceding one. Possibly the second set were for repeated performances at which he, not
Barbara, was the soloist. The climax of all this loveliness comes after
the cadenza, in a short coda with the same two elements—chromati-
cism followed by the patient resignation of the major key (Ex. 93). It

seems strange that this wonderful movement, open to those of us who are far poorer players than Fräulein Ployer, is so little known.

3. *Finale, Allegretto*

The last movement brings us again to the atmosphere of comic opera, and claims our attention because in all previous concertos

94.

95.

96.

Mozart wrote the customary rondo-finale. The tune, or at least a version of its first quarter, was endeared to Mozart by a pet starling (Ex. 94). But most of us will be reminded of another bird who was half a man, and whose songs might well have included the whole tune: I refer, of course, to Papageno in the *Magic Flute*.

The movement consists of five variations upon this tune, one or two of which move farther from the original than do any variations by previous composers except J. S. Bach. Barbara must have had to work hard at the triplets, especially the left-hand strophes of the second variation, unless the piece was taken much more slowly than we take it nowadays. Most of these variations have already been discussed in Chapter IV, and there is no need to spend much space upon them here. The last variation, if such it can be called, is so unusual as to make the whole piece unique. Without it, the movement would be too short, and as it is there is no shorter set of variations in all the concertos; but the peculiar final presto is calculated to give perfect satisfaction and to extort applause from the most disapproving sobersides. The penultimate variation gives a chain of the favourite seven-six suspensions, magically exploited (Ex. 95), its caprice changing to loveliness in a cadence of supreme beauty, unthinkable from any other composer. Anything may happen; a variation in keeping with that cadence? No: not in a finale built upon the starling tune. Instead we are taken presto into the land of comic opera from which the concerto began its journey (Ex. 96), and the movement finishes in the sauciest manner known in any concerto.

This finale is seen to be unique in construction; five variations only are followed by a lengthy final section that cannot be regarded as a variation. The variations themselves are of superb quality, but the final section, with its comic spirit and the capricious, starling-like scrappets of the theme, could not have completed one of the finest of Mozart's concerto finales had it been shorter. It is difficult not to suppose that Mozart took special care about the length and order of the textures that compose this movement, for the peculiarity of structure goes with a peculiarity of mood. Many a finale is playful; many a finale seeks merely to enchant and entertain; but Mozart very rarely allowed his music to express that degree of incongruity, indulged by Haydn and Beethoven, which makes us speak of humour rather than wit. The starling tune, especially in the twittering form it takes when last quoted, crosses the borderline between wit and humour, and Mozart may have been at pains to ensure that flippant material should not bring an accusation of flippant treatment; the high quality of the variations, seen in the pathetic austerity quoted at Ex. 30 and 31, or the haunting beauty quoted at Ex. 95, together with the perfectly planned length of the final section—these seem to bear witness to unusual care. Why should there be any such solicitude?

The expression of humour in music is fraught with danger; it is rarely successful, though Beethoven's work alone testifies to its possibility in the hands of genius. If the music is to be at a high level, the humour must be of a simple order, and it will surely be agreed that, however high the level of Beethoven's scherzi, their humour is of the simplest. A few moments reflection will show the reason for this. Humour is our defence when we contemplate the incongruities of our nature and experience, and humorists are those who use life's incongruities for their material and commentary. The greater the incongruity, the better the joke for those whose deeper feelings are not affected. The sudden fall of a dignitary in procession is more amusing than the fall of a footballer during a game, unless our personal affection for the victim, or our deep allegiance to the institution he represents, becomes outraged at the mishap. It will be seen that perfection of form, the congruity of parts within a whole, is the primary quality of any music worth hearing, and that any composer, whatever his powers, risks the perfection of his music when he handles the material of humour, unless some pictorial or literary programme explains caprice and incongruity. Had the story of the pet starling become well known to Mozart's first audience?

Whatever the answer to that question, Mozart ensured that this finale should have congruity as a whole and unusual wit in its parts, and so commend itself to the most sober listener. If the materials of humour are taken from humanity itself, those of wit are taken from the medium of expression. The literary wit plays with words; the musical wit with musical technique. The parallels to verbal witticisms are enharmonic modulations, syncopated rhythms, overlapping phrases, and displays of skill which surprise us by their beauty. Musical wit excites our admiration and wonder, and that is why the finale to K. 453 is not likely to raise a smile from the most fatuous of listeners, except perhaps at the mock pomposity which follows the double bar between the variations and the final section, or at the hurried and jerky bird-like fragments of the tune which interrupt the last bars of that section. In these places alone does the movement step from wit to humour, and to justify them the composer surrounds them with musical wit and musical seriousness of a very high order.

CHAPTER XI

CONCERTO IN B FLAT, K. 456

CONCERTO IN B FLAT, K. 456. *Completed by 30 September 1784*
1. Allegro vivace, 4/4.
2. Andante un poco sostenuto, 2/4. Variations upon a theme in G minor.
3. Allegro vivace, 6/8.

Orchestra: As in previous concerto; strings, one flute, two oboes, two bassoons, two horns.

Biographical notes

1. *Letter from Leopold Mozart to his daughter, written during his stay with the composer in Vienna:*

'On Sunday evening . . . your brother played a glorious concerto, which he composed for Mdlle. Paradis for Paris. I was sitting only two boxes away from the very beautiful Princess of Wurtemberg and had the great pleasure of hearing so clearly all the interplay of the instruments, that for sheer delight the tears came into my eyes. When your brother left the platform, the Emperor waved his hat and called out "Bravo Mozart!" and when he came on to play, there was a great deal of clapping.'

2. Maria Theresa Paradies was a Viennese performer, blind from birth. During 1784 she undertook a tour of European capitals. Special intimacy with the Mozarts may have grown during the previous year, when the visit of the newly married couple to Leopold happened to coincide with the blind pianist's appearance in Salzburg.[1]

THE fourth, fifth, and sixth concertos of this *annus mirabilis* may far more reasonably be regarded as forming a group than may the first three which are often spoken of as a trio, either because of a sentence in one of Mozart's letters, or because they were all composed within a few weeks of March–April 1784. But the second three, of which the composition was spread over the remaining months of the year, show a marked consolidation of first-movement structure; each uses the same size of orchestra, and each has other points in common with the

---

[1] K. 456 may not have been the concerto for Paradies, and she cannot have played it in Paris during 1784. See Hermann Ullrich's essay in *Music and Letters*, vol. xxvii, no. 4.

other two, even to such details as the opening rhythmic figure. These points will be discussed as they occur in the several movements.

1. *First Movement, Allegro Vivace*

The concertos of 1784 are the first entries into Mozart's newly

kept note-book catalogue; in that book he must have seen the similar rhythms with which the last three concertos of that year open. See Ex. 97.

But the differences between these very themes, once we carry them forward to the next phrase, are as important as their similarities, for they initiate a wide contrast in feeling between the concertos. The last one, in F, has a proud swagger which marks a brilliant, masculine work written for the composer himself. It comes nearer in spirit to the difficult B flat Concerto of the previous trio (K. 450) than it does to either of its neighbours. We are left, therefore, to compare the openings of the first two. It must be noted that these themes are not Great First Subjects as in Beethoven; they are trifles which serve but one structural purpose, viz. to open their concertos, and mark the point of recapitulation. Yet in the G major opening, the sequential imitation of rhythm is delayed till four bars have passed, the theme being extended to contain two elements. The B flat theme is only two short bars in length; the rhythm repeats in the next two bars and another type of texture follows. Here, then, is the chief difference between Barbara Ployer's concerto and this one in B flat; all the elements in the later concerto are on a smaller scale. Among the mature concertos, this could most easily be called a toy concerto. However consistently the themes are contrasted, however intrinsically expressive, they seem to be miniatures of those heard somewhere else in Mozart, so crisp and child-like are they (Exx. 98–100).

As we play this delightful movement—and it is an excellent one to play at home, whether there is a second piano or not—we cannot fail to notice that this work was written between *The Seraglio* and *Figaro*; consequently it has much in common with the preceding G major Concerto. Theme C, heard in prelude, exposition, and reprise, has the moodiness and shiftiness of operatic writing (Ex. 101). Theme D takes us to the garden scene in *Figaro* and in Exx. 102–3 we see the reason why.

If the list of unaccountably shelved Mozart concertos is headed by K. 449 in E flat, this K. 456 should come next, on account of the wonderful slow movement. It is strongly commended to the home pianist since it is easy to read, easy to remember, and grateful to the fingers; the only difficulty is to play it cleanly and crisply and to know when to give it the warmth of the sustaining pedal. If Mozart wrote it for Paradies, he gave her every facility in memorizing; his themes are clearly articulated and contrasted.

Elsewhere one has spoken about Mozart's 'conventionality', and about the right and wrong use of that word. One might try an experiment upon those who use it wrongly. Play the first two bars of the movement we are studying, and ask the examinee to supply the next two bars, since the phrase is 'mere stock-in-trade'. We shall then see

that even in paltry details Mozart is personal; the candidate is not likely to turn the complementary phrase upwards, and he will certainly not slip in the G at bar four. There will be a dull and conventional six-three chord instead of the G-against-F discord (Ex. 97*b*).

2. *Second Movement, Andante un poco sostenuto*

This set of variations has already been discussed in Chapter IV. There is nothing to add here except that the tune gives us another reminder of *Figaro*, a memory of Barbarina searching for the lost pin, again in the garden scene. Despite the intense poignance of this movement, Mozart preserves the 'toy' character of the whole concerto, even in the theme itself.

3. *Third Movement, Allegro Vivace*

Still a concerto of miniatures! Still 'toy' tunes! How one wishes for the older type of piano, with the lighter action and more metallic tone, on which to play these tunes of repeated notes! The orchestral music following the main rondo themes seems to come straight from the pages of modern light music (Ex. 104).

After a rattle of symmetrical rondo tunes and keyboard figurations, just as the sobersides are thinking this a somewhat superficial piece, comes a surprise of some audacity. In 2/4 time against the continued 6/8 of the strings (Ex. 105) the solo reverts to the pathetic world of the previous movement, and in B minor of all unforeseen keys. To have broken into a minuet, as in the Salzburg E flat Concerto, K. 271, was at least something to public taste; but this B minor stroke is unprecedented. The return to the toyshop is equally sudden (Ex. 106).

Mozart left two cadenzas for the first movement, the second being perhaps for his own performances. It is more brilliant but less attractive than the first cadenza, which contains a new chromatic treatment of Ex. 98 (quoted at Ex. 107). There is also a cadenza for the Finale.

CHAPTER XII

CONCERTO IN F, K. 459

CONCERTO IN F, K. 459. *Finished by 11 December 1784*
1. Allegro, 4/4.
2. Allegretto, 6/8, in C major.
3. Allegro, 2/4.
Orchestra: Strings, one flute, two oboes, two bassoons, two horns.

Biographical notes

The same letter from Leopold Mozart to his daughter, quoted on page 114, continues: 'We were not at the theatre yesterday, for every day there is a concert. This evening there is another in the theatre, at which your brother is again playing a concerto. I shall bring back several of his new compositions.' This F major is the last concerto of 1784.

THE F major Concerto is a joyous and popular work; moodiness does not cloud one of its movements, yet there is no superficial writing. There are one or two concertos in which a happy but simpering rondo, or a languid, shallow, slow movement, falls short of the excellence of its preceding movement. The F major Concerto gives us first-rate Mozart through each of its radiant movements; its smile is quite unsentimental, and implies no complementary tears. It is a work which, since it combines vigour and grace, may well be called athletic.

1. *First Movement, Allegro*

At last we reach a movement in which it is difficult to find the influence of the theatre. Not since the fully orchestrated D major, K. 451, has there been a movement so symphonic, so essentially instrumental, as this one. Though quite different in spirit from Beethoven's writing, the texture of this movement shows an approach to Beethovenian methods such as is not seen before in the series of concertos, and is rarely seen afterwards. It has already been observed that this concerto has the same rhythm in its initial bar as have its two predecessors, with this difference, that here the rhythm dominates the movement. Theme A (see page 115) is still the first of six in a highly organized orchestral prelude, but as the movement proceeds, 'A' dominates the others; it marches in as a ritornello by the orchestra, it is used sequentially or contrapuntally like a Beethovenian development; its rhythm punctuates other themes, thrusting itself into tenor or alto, into a horn or bassoon staccato—in fact, 165 bars of a movement containing 400 show the presence either of this theme or of its rhythm, and there is further reference to it in one of Mozart's most brilliant cadenzas. Here is the plan to scale:

		No. of bars	Bars with 'A'
Prelude	A | B | C | D | E | F	72	16
Exposition	A | B | x | A | y | A ▨ D ▨	116	54
First ritornello	A | G | A | G	22	12
Middle section	H | A | H | A | H | A	35	12
Recapitulation	A | B | A | y | A | D | A ▨	116	62
Final ritornello	A | G | A | Cadenza | E | F	32	9

(Shaded parts represent free passages, largely occupied with fast scales and arpeggios in triplet measure.)

The reader who has hitherto passed over the diagrams is asked to study this one, comparing it with the diagrams of other concertos. Structural problems are not the main point of interest even when studying a unique evolution of one form through the work of one man. Here, however, a structural development not only gives special impress upon the character of the concerto, but foretells important changes during Mozart's last years as a concertist. The structure cannot be regarded separately from other elements, such as the nature of the themes themselves, for just as the juxtaposed moods, the shiftiness and modulations of the E flat Concerto, K. 449, or the G major, K. 453, gave those works an operatic atmosphere, so directly opposite methods give this F major Concerto its brilliantly symphonic and athletic nature.

We have noted the predominance of A and of its rhythm. We may count almost as many bars in which occurs the triplet rhythm of D;

when the two cross, as in Ex. 108, we have one of the chief contributions to the symphonic weaving and sturdiness of the piece. Remove
ritornelli and we have Mozart's nearest approach yet to the symphonic
type of concerto, presaged by the aridly brilliant D major, K. 451.
Whereas none of the five subjects of the prelude plays anything but
a ritornellic part, the theme labelled y is plainly *the* symphonic second

108.

109.

subject, in a manner more marked than hitherto. Since it is no more
than a tune it is not developed, but is used for contrast with the
closer-knit and ubiquitous first-subject texture.

Omit ritornelli and cadenza and we have an approximation *in
expository structure* to the first movement of Beethoven's symphonies
and concertos, though Mozart does not abandon the concerto principles he has consolidated, such as the refusal to make a plain recapitulation of his expository material. The second subject, y, to which
we have just alluded, is one of those apparently simple gems which
are cunningly ornamented and extended by the slipping in of extra
measures which prevent symmetry (Ex. 109).

2. *Second Movement, Allegretto*

It has been remarked that this concerto is consistent. The radiance of first movement and Finale is shared by this idyll with its quiet 6/8 swing. It is not built in strophes, but broadly speaking in 'short sonata' form without middle section, having an orchestral prelude and coda derived from its main sonata theme.

The first pleasant surprise for a newcomer to this movement is the asymmetrical overlapping of phrases (Ex. 110 and 111). The second is the delicious interplay of wood-wind with strings and solo, especially at the end of the movement, which is reminiscent of 'Deh vieni', in *Figaro* (Ex. 112). But for these two features we should be aware of the plain recapitulation, with new key adjustment, which pre-Beethovenian composers did not recognize as a weakness. A plain AB : AB movement, like the Andante of the 'Haffner' Symphony, is inclined to tax modern patience, as do the repeats of minuet and trio. But Mozart's second subject or paragraph, being in a minor key, and showing slight variation at its reprise, maintains the interest.

This is the first appearance of a middle movement to a Mozart concerto which is marked Allegretto; it is as surely the right movement in the right place as is the Allegretto of another athletic work in F major—Beethoven's Eighth Symphony.

3. *Finale, Allegro assai*

This is one of Mozart's greatest and most entertaining rondos; that the adjectives used rarely make a pair we have remarked before, and Mozart was well aware of the fact.

'These concertos are a happy medium between what is too easy and too difficult; they are very brilliant, pleasing to the ear, and natural without being vapid. Here and there are passages from which connoisseurs alone can derive satisfaction; but these passages are written in such a way that the less learned cannot fail to be pleased, though without knowing why.'

All this applies as much to the Rondo of K. 459 as it does to the first Vienna concertos to which Mozart referred.

The chief contributors to this magnificent finale are the technical effects which distinguish the concerto as a whole:

1. Extensive use of a clearly marked first theme, which is a good deal more than a refrain.
2. Contrast of its smiling homophony with passages of counterpoint—not just the cross-rhythm of the first movement, but a fully developed fugato paragraph (Ex. 113).

There follows a tutti of sufficient length, importance, and diversity to constitute the orchestral prelude to a Mozartian first movement, and indeed this finale is architecturally on the scale of a first movement; of all Mozart's finales it has most claim to the title 'sonata

110.

111.

112.

rondo', if by that we mean a movement in which there is a closer relation between sections than the contrasts of refrain, episodes, and Mozartian extra tunes.

A few words should be said here about Mozart's counterpoint. When sixteenth-century polyphony came to its autumn, despite the Indian summer of Gibbons in England and Bach in Germany, composers no longer thought in 'points', or musical phrases to be

'countered'. The older musicians guided themselves by making con-
cord or suspension on main accents, and by superimposing intervals
above the first written part; but their eyes looked horizontally when
doing this. Once their generation died, and metricized dance measures cast an influence even over the choruses of cantatas, composers
who sought the stiffening qualities of counterpoint approached their
study as do so many students to-day, from a harmonic point of view
—and a very bad point of view it is after the first few lessons, which
seem necessary when students have first been taught harmony from
a chordal aspect. It makes them acquire obedience without style,
and write counterpoint as bad as Beethoven's without the compensation of Beethoven's genius.[1]

Between a Bach chorus or chorale-prelude and a canto-fermo mass
of the polyphonic age, there is far less in common than some teachers
tell their pupils (if they train their pupils to write like Bach). Teachers
are more honest if they declare that they teach decoration and texture.
If one sets up as a teacher of counterpoint, one should train along the
lines of invention seen in the development of musical history—first
discant, then florid counterpoint, imitative and free, then the Palestrinian contrast of textures (some clearly homophonic), then the art
of the string fantasia and madrigal. The Viennese masters, to a man,
felt the need of contrapuntal study when they were already composers
of repute, and it is pretty certain that though they learnt nothing from
their teachers (we still have Fuxes and Albrechtsbergers among us!)
they learnt a good deal for themselves while doing the set tasks. If
Beethoven's counterpoint shows any marked improvement after his
lessons, then where do we find it? There exist good counterpoint
teachers, but they are still not so well recognized as those who give a
student what he pays the fees to get, namely, a pass at a musical
examination; for when the examiners are not the teachers, they are
former pupils of the same teachers.

The one word which one cannot find from most counterpoint
teachers, or from standard treatises on counterpoint, is 'style'. Mozart
and Schubert, who by nature were quickly absorbent and perceptive
of style, made better contrapuntists than the sturdy, more self-centred
and self-absorbed Beethoven. Beethoven wore the contrapuntal dress
awkwardly, even when the implied harmony was of the simplest, for
only a clever perceiver of style can hide the harmonic approach.

---

[1] I speak of Beethoven's *formal* counterpoint. Of the art of cross-rhythm,
granted metrical pulse, he was such a master that one wonders what he sought
from academic counterpoint.

Cherubini's worked exercises would disgrace any intelligent counterpoint student; they contain not one piece of texture which Palestrina
would have called music or counterpoint, and if Cherubini had been
a teacher of genuine counterpoint his treatise would have contained

113.

114.

115.

very few worked exercises; instead it would have been filled with
examples from Lassus, Palestrina, Byrd, and Vittoria. Martini,
greatest of teachers, professed only 'music'.

Mozart would never have regarded Cherubini's worked examples
as music, but we need not suppose that Mozart knew any more about
the contrapuntal method of approach to music than did Cherubini.
What he did know and admire, and what few of his contemporaries

knew in a rococo age, was the baroque contrapuntal style of Bach.
He arranged some of the 'Forty-eight' for strings; at St. Thomas's,
Leipzig, when he improvised on the organ, it was declared that such
music had not been heard there since Bach died; he studied the music
of Bach and Handel and arranged it for Van Swieten's 'academies',[1]
and Constanze encouraged him to write fugues—perhaps they kept
him out of mischief. But Mozart saw as a series of harmonies, made
into stronger and more noble texture by appoggiaturas and suspensions what to Palestrina came from countering points.

Thus Ex. 114, from the Kyrie of the C minor Mass, one of the
most glorious things written by Mozart, is harmony magnificently
decorated. The older polyphonists made beauty by protracting
resolution of discord. Mozart loved the mild discords for their own
sake, and towards the end of his life they were not always mild. A
well-known passage from *Figaro* shows one of them on the first beat
of each bar (Ex. 115).

Mozart's abnormal receptiveness gave him the most complete grasp
that has yet been known of that diatonic system which is the basis of
European musical training. This may seem an extravagant claim,
but we can explain many a Mozartian *tour de force* only by recognizing
that the man could carry in his head not just chords, their inversions,
and a few stock 'contrapuntal' gambits—for these served all musicians
of talent—but the discords, suspensions, and contrapuntal ornaments
which most of us, even to-day, have to work out, as we do a mathe-
matical problem. We could not use them in extempore playing, as he
did. A passage like Ex. 116, from the D major Quintet, not a particularly ambitious work, could have been written by no other composer, ancient or modern. Yet its movement opens tamely and
serenely and is not disturbed by this writing itself. To hear the passage without seeing it on the score paper, is to be unaware of its
astounding technical virtuosity. Thus easily does Mozart seem to
have acquired the style; this is a measure of his superb taste.

Because such texture was acquired by diligent study, and because
he delighted in discord and its resolution, his fugues, such as the
C minor for two pianos, or the great 'Quam olim Abrahae' in the
Requiem, are tougher than the average Bach fugue. This study and
this delight in contrapuntal technique enabled him to combine such
texture with homophonic ideas. Hence the 'Jupiter' Finale, the
Finale of the G major Quartet, and the Finale to the F major Piano

[1] i.e. concerts of what was called Ancient Music.

Concerto, to the study of which we must return (Ex. 119).

The many homophonic tunes illustrate the quality which must come from nature, not from study, namely, invention, by which a blundering genius may remain a living composer while a conscientious and faultless talent is forgotten. However inspired the texture, no man can write counterpoint without planning his rhythms ahead, without synthetic invention, so to speak. To write a good plain and

entertaining tune, which will attract with nothing but a homophonic
background, or with no background at all, there must be rhythmic
vitality. The expectation of life wagered on a mere ephemeral song
or dance depends on its catchiness, *allure*, novelty, in which rhythm
plays a large part, though in the best tunes it is an integral part of the
melodic invention. When Leopold rose on the morning after his son
had played the F major Concerto, four catchy tunes might have been

119.

going through his head, of which Ex. 117 is only one, though the
invention sparkles right through the piece to its final cadences
(Ex. 118).

Thus, side by side in this excellent Finale, we see Mozart the
natural genius, and Mozart the superb contrapuntal and structural
craftsman. But we must be careful with the word 'counterpoint'.
Bar 8 of Ex. 119 would not be allowed by academic contrapuntists.
Mozart has to add parts to make smooth the progression of parts
already existing, though this smoothing is not the thick application
of harmonic paste which makes possible the famous combination of
motives in the *Mastersingers* Prelude. Like many a composer already

in brilliant mastery of his own personal music, Mozart strove for further mastery in counterpoint; but let us rid ourselves of the supposition that, had he known the masterpieces of Palestrina, he would have understood them or valued them. We already know the small worth of Wagner's praise of Palestrina; we also know that, despite preparatory exercises from Padre Martini, Mozart failed in the counterpoint examination for membership of the Bologna Accademia Filarmonica. Martini's corrections to Mozart's vocal parts gained the boy a 'bare pass'. I believe that such passages as Ex. 119 were not written easily.

CHAPTER XIII

CONCERTO IN D MINOR, K. 466

CONCERTO IN D MINOR, K. 466. *Completed by 10 February 1785*
1. Allegro, 4/4.
2. Romanza in B flat, 4/4.
3. Rondo: Allegro assai, 4/4.

Orchestra: Strings, one flute, two oboes, two bassoons, two horns, two trumpets, two drums.

Biographical notes

This concerto was selected for examination in Chapter I, since no concerto by Mozart is better known; for many generations it has enjoyed this popularity. Leopold Mozart liked it so much that he tried to perform it with a circle of musical friends in Salzburg, and wrote to tell Wolfgang of his difficulties with the text. Young Beethoven's fine cadenzas are now almost as sacrosanct as the main concerto, and as there are no original cadenzas available there seems no reason for substituting any other effort for Beethoven's, unless one is a purist and plays a very short extemporization and a shake.

1. *First Movement, Allegro*

THE sinister syncopations which open the movement make it vibrate with nervous energy; we feel their smouldering fire to be continually beneath any passing melody. It bursts out in other themes of the first movement (see Exx. 6 and 7 above) in the middle of the romanza, and finally in the first long orchestral tutti of the Rondo (Ex. 120).

A deal of nonsense gets written in programme notes about this concerto, and cussedness tempts one to give no further account of the spiritual content of the D minor than: 'This is the first of the series in a minor key, which to western ears is not predisposed to hilarity; C. P. E. Bach wrote several concertos in a minor key. Mozart's concerto is otherwise normal.' But Superior Persons cannot honestly let the D minor Concerto go with that; the work is unlike any other by Mozart and unlike any concerto by other composers. It comes as a surprise.

120.

121.

122.

The only way to account for that surprise is to admit that there is no *obvious* correspondence between Mozart's inner and outer life; we may know facts about his debts and digestion but we cannot correlate them with his key signatures, because we do not know how long the conception of a work like this took in his mind before it appeared in the concerto series. We exclaim with Blake: 'Did he who made the lamb make thee?' Those of us who are impatient with romantic vapourings feel the same admiration as do the romantics, but our wonder is like Blake's dread and wonder at the Tiger—it is concentrated on the word 'symmetry'. That word expresses the difference we note between K. 466 and the C minor Symphony of Beethoven. Moreover, we see an asset, not a limitation, in the classical wealth and ritornello-organization which constantly holds the passion of the D minor Concerto in leash.

Girdlestone gives considerable space to a repudiation of short-eared persons who think the D minor 'Beethovenian' and suppose that their thinking so is a compliment to Mozart. The D minor Concerto is no more like Beethoven than the 'Little Eighth' Symphony is like Mozart. Of the concerto Beethoven would not have written a single theme, not a single bar—not even the cadential bars.

2. *Romanza*

The little phrase quoted at Ex. 121 occurs fourteen times, and for one pair of ears that is six times too often. The melody which makes the refrain-in-full a ternary form is graceful and limpid, but it is not particularly inspired. Mozart at his most pedestrian, like Pope, was such a master of the craft of his age that his stock-in-trade becomes enjoyable to audiences with whom it has the charm of a fragrant past.

The galloping G minor portion of this Romanza sounds like an attempt to shake the music from the enervation of the refrain.

3. *Rondo, allegro assai*

This magnificent movement has been fully examined in Chapter I. Two aspects of it need discussion. First, it differs from the opening movement in that the orchestral instruments are more exposed; the scoring for the wind instruments is more like that in other concertos, whereas the scoring of the first movement is symphonic. The nervous syncopations and the angry tremolo in the first movement depend entirely on string technique; the trumpets make no fanfare, the drums no paradiddle; they add nothing but sombre colour. The most temperamental first movement before that of the D minor Concerto was the opening one of K. 449 in E flat, and it is noteworthy that Mozart

123.

124.

125.

scored K. 449 in such a way that all wind instruments could be omitted. Some sort of performance of K. 466 could be given with strings only, provided the performance stopped at the end of the first movement. A most delicious change in scoring occurs just after the cadenza of the last movement, when we expect a return of the rondo refrain in D minor, and are treated instead to the sunniest of all the subsidiary themes, presented in D major and comically prepared by the bassoons (Ex. 122).

Extreme classicists have wished that this rondo ended symmetrically in D minor; extreme romanticists have wished that the heart be kept bleeding to the last drop; but for most musicians who have once enjoyed the D major coda, no other conclusion seems possible. Despite the minor key, this is not a troubled movement; its spirit is of grim, masculine vigour, unusual in Mozart. If ever that composer set out to be deliberately witty in pure music, he did so at the trumpet entry quoted at Ex. 14.

CHAPTER XIV

CONCERTO IN C, K. 467

CONCERTO IN C MAJOR, K. 467. *Completed by 9 March 1785*
1. Allegro maestoso, 4/4.
2. Andante (in F), 4/4.
3. Allegro vivace assai, 2/4.

Orchestra: Strings, one flute, two oboes, two bassoons, two horns, two trumpets, two drums.

Biographical notes

Letter of Leopold Mozart, 14 January 1786: 'Indeed the new concerto is astonishingly difficult. But I very much doubt whether there are any mistakes, as the copyist has checked it. Several passages simply do not harmonise unless one hears all the instruments playing together.' Since K. 467 was written four weeks after K. 466, there is no biographical material to add to that which concerns the former concerto.

OF Mozart's four concertos in C major, this is the most consistently satisfactory, although the first movement of the later K. 503 is among the greatest of all concerto movements. K. 467 is also among the composer's most joyful works: tenderness is found in the dream world of its andante but the tenderness is without introspection. The first movement has the strut of the march which brings down the first curtain in *Figaro*, and the finale is as merry as the steam organ of which it undoubtedly reminds modern listeners—and possibly did contemporary ones, without the steam.

1. *First Movement, Allegro maestoso*

It would be interesting to ask one who is not very familiar with the Mozart concertos to name the composer of Ex. 123. His answer would probably be 'Schumann'. Its Schumannesque suavity and *Schwärmerei* is Mozart's chosen means to offset the marching tunes which dominate the first movement. The passage I have quoted occurs in the first orchestral ritornello. We who are used to Schumann's sweet piquancies, his unprepared sevenths, the added sixths

and seconds which are no longer regarded as discords since they are
the small change of commercial music, cannot be expected to recognize the extent to which Mozart enriched the musical vocabulary of
galanterie; we note the acid minor seconds of the D minor or C minor
Concertos, because those are disturbing works, but Leopold's letter
(mentioned in the biographical note to this concerto) is that of an
indulgent father who obviously wonders whether such things as
unprepared seconds are allowed in the vocabulary of a composer of
Good Taste.

To us, K. 467 is one of those happy works which provide the last
hunting grounds for discord; but it is rather more than that. One
cannot but reckon it as one of Mozart's technical triumphs, for in it
we see the achievement of a promise. The previous concerto in the
same key showed only promise.

That work, K. 415, has a similar conception and similar parts—a
conspiratorially quiet, staccato march, a brave forte passage to follow,
then lyricism like that just quoted; indeed its parts are hardly less
fine than those of K. 467, and our disappointment lies in the fact that
they are greater than the whole. The opening march becomes an
irritant when it turns up from place to place in the same battledress;
the *fugato* was hardly suitable for ritornellic purposes and in K. 467
the *fugato* is wisely given only one presentation as ritornello. Mozart's
mature wisdom is seen at the very opening, where the march, not
announced *fugato*, is followed by a homophonic theme before it
appears as bass to the forte texture (Ex. 125).

At first hearing of this genial movement one is surprised that it
follows the passionate D minor Concerto within four weeks; certainly
one would be surprised to know that it is hardly less highly organized
than the first movement of its predecessor; the structural mastery of
K. 467 is less obvious than that of K. 466 because its texture does not
show the same degree of tension. The D minor is among the most
closely packed of concertos; there is hardly a bar of pianistic *bravura*
which does not interplay with an orchestral theme, or does not refer
to a main theme of its own. In the following concerto, however,
there is happy time and ample room for plenty of virtuosic writing
in between tunes; and what an advance the keyboard *bravura* shows!
While we know the march-theme is ready to stalk into the scene,
subsidiary tunes that happen to hold the stage are the idlest progeny
of summer, and only Mozart could put them in a concerto without
insipidity or banality (Ex. 126).

One of the eight tunes found in this movement is almost identical with the first subject of Mozart's great G minor Symphony, having by coincidence the same key; but it is a poor capture for a spook-hunter since, as a 'new' tune for the solo exposition, it occurs only the once.

126.

127.

128.

Of more interest are the brilliant reshuffle and condensation of materials for the reprise, and the charming, unusual way in which the solo seems to be led by the hand on to its platform. At first it is all coyness (Ex. 127). It needs asking three times to begin its performance, but the hypocrite seeks by such behaviour to enhance the

129.

brilliance shown within a few bars of the opening. This playful
conduct is symbolic of the whole concerto. In the D minor Concerto

the entry was a direct statement, coming immediately after the orchestral cadence, and with the very theme which the orchestra had never to play. The essence of the D minor Concerto is dramatic opposition or juxtaposition; the first subjects heard by orchestra and solo respectively are seen as two protagonists, though in that tight texture every bar is functional to dramatic structure. The D minor has no place for coyness, speechifying, or skylarking. The C major is an entertainment; to continue the metaphor, we may call it a pageant or a revue, but we must not be blind to the fact that its scenes, so loosely strung, its side-shows and its brilliant spectacles, make a whole which is as much a work of genius as is the more imposing, more Shakespearian, D minor.

2. *Second Movement, Andante*

A conception of melody is found among certain nineteenth-century composers that shows no love of metrical rhythm, nor of the antithesis of similar phrases, but derives its form from tension it engenders within itself. In Bergsonian phrase, the form is 'a becoming'. In it we may be aware of phrases, of sequences which show metabolism or which gather other germs as their own germs burgeon; but the main principle of its form is the approach to and decline from climax, there being one big and several small points of climax in a long melody. We call such writing rhapsodic. Mozart's most captivating tunes are cunningly articulated, but their beauty is sufficiently of its static, classical period for the *eye* to take some part in appreciation. We can analyse his melody without, as Wordsworth says, 'murdering to dissect'. As we listen to it, we can 'cast an eye' over it, whereas while listening to rhapsody we imagine ourselves to be the performer; if we do not live along its line, we are not fulfilling the composer's demands of us.

Something very near to later rhapsodic melody is found in the flowing traceries with which Bach adorned his finest chorale-preludes; in the slow movement of many a concerto by the same master, embellishment becomes—with a player who is not a charlatan—something more than a compendium of ornaments, and the melody, which else had clanked along beneath the weight of adventitious riches, acquires a rhapsodic fluidity which makes the performer feel the constant need to control his rhythm and expression. (The effort is a great test of artistry and a powerful source of emotion.) In one type of slow movement alone do we find Mozart, of all people, approaching the free melody of the rhapsodists; the andante of K. 467 is the last specimen among the concertos. It is also the best, for examples of the type are rare among any of Mozart's mature works. He was fonder of what Girdlestone calls the 'dream-andante' or 'reverie' in his younger days, using it in more than one symphony and chamber work as well as in piano concertos of the Salzburg period. One's own favourite is the beautiful example, whose opening is quoted on page 51, from the little B flat Concerto, K. 238, but perhaps the best known instance of its use is in the G major Violin Concerto, for the rhapsodic dream-andante seems most happily suited to the violin with string accompaniment.

If we took the trouble to write out elements of the various themes in K. 467 which recur in the andante, we should find the whole movement to be a big binary form with two main groups of subject-matter in the usual keys; but the effort would be tedious and of little musical value. What is of more interest is to note the means by which we are lured into a dream world. The orchestral introduction, lasting seven bars, is no parade of ritornello material; its muted strings are like those sounding while the curtain slowly rises, and we see as through a gauze the golden radiance of the fields of sleep. (Blom does no dishonour to Mozart by his dictum, of which one is constantly aware in the piano concertos: 'Here we enter a world of enchanted artificiality.') The soft recalcitrancy of triplets against the quadruple time of the melody—a texture which is maintained throughout the movement—tells us that this world of phantasm is inhabited (Ex. 128). The solo begins, and passes from phrase to unequal phrase, with many a mood and many a modulation yet never with any sudden, dramatic, or momentous change of key, time, or mood. If there is something of the aria about its sustained lyricism, then that aria is narrative; it is neither the unified and subjective elaboration of one emotion which we find in the aria of Mozartian opera, or in the later pianoforte nocturnes of Field and Chopin, nor is it quite the narrative aria which we find in *Madame Butterfly* or *Norma*. Yet it is not one of Gluck's blessed spirits that is telling its life-story from the other side of the gauze. Mozart's spirit is an operatic character with a human soul, and no supernatural personage of Apolline art.

The scoring is very unusual. It is in fact unique, as may be seen from the quotation from the full score made at Ex. 129. An asterisk has been placed over the first violin part to show the kind of discord which troubled Leopold (the B flat against the B natural) but which gives us such pleasure.

3. *Finale, Allegro vivace assai*

This movement is as unusual in its conformity with text-book sonata-rondo as it is usual in being witty and loosely joined. The solo enters with an impish stamp, Ex. 130, and pose, and then pirouettes to its repetition of the rondo tune. At the pace intended, the repetitions and sequences cannot weary.

The wind writing at the beginning of the extract quoted at Ex. 130 shows the fair-organ spirit of the piece, as do little passages like Ex. 131. Other parts justify one's use of a balletomane's vocabulary. Ex. 132 recalls a Sadlers Wells favourite—surely one of the dances from *Prometheus*; and that sets us hunting out quite a number of rhythms used by Beethoven in his more unbuttoned middle-period rondos, as for example Exx. 133 and 134.

Analysis would be simple and unnecessary, like a lecture given to boys at the entrance gate of a fair-ground, telling them how best to lay out their pennies upon the delights within.

CHAPTER XV

CONCERTO IN E FLAT, K. 482

CONCERTO IN E FLAT, K. 482. *Completed by 16 December 1785*
1. Allegro, 4/4.
2. Andante, in C minor, 3/8.
3. Allegro, 6/8, with andante episode, 3/4.

Orchestra: Strings, one flute, two clarinets, two bassoons, two horns, two
trumpets, two drums.

Biographical notes

The fact that there is no concerto between March and December
1785 shows that K. 467 and K. 482 were written for two winter
seasons, public concerts being few in the summer months when 'the
quality' withdrew to the country. After the 1784-5 concert season,
Mozart devoted himself to more intimate works than concertos. The
six quartets needed completion; by August they were dedicated and
sent off to Haydn. Work then began upon *Figaro*.

When Leopold Mozart was staying with Wolfgang and Constanze
in 1785, he wrote to his daughter, telling her of Haydn's famous
tribute to Mozart's genius and of the quartet playing with Haydn,
Dittersdorf, and Vanhall. In January 1786, that is to say, in the
middle of the new concert season, Leopold wrote: 'I have had a reply
from your brother in which he says that he gave without much
preparation three subscription concerts to 120 subscribers, that he
composed for this purpose a new piano concerto in E flat, in which
[a rather unusual occurrence!] he had to repeat the andante.'

1. *First movement, Allegro*

THOSE who like to be sententious may think of K. 482 as the 'concerto
with clarinets'; it was thus that Tovey thought of the big E flat
Symphony which he described as 'the *locus classicus* for euphony'.
Had Mozart left no symphonies (in which case the concertos might
have been adequately studied) K. 482 might well have enjoyed
Tovey's description of the symphony. When Mozart uses trumpets
and drums in the key of E flat they have not the masculine bravado
of D and C major; in this concerto they give grandeur and dignity
to the opening minim but indulge in no military fanfares. The gracious lyricism, the great length of the first movement, the use of
clarinets instead of oboes,[1] the absence of hurry or petulance, the

---

[1] Two oboists, who played clarinets when asked, would use their titular instruments when clarinets were not available, but there is no excuse for oboes in a
modern performance. See Carse's *The Orchestra in the Eighteenth Century*.

number of tunes—all these make the Venus of Mozartian concerto movements, whose character has more than one family resemblance to that of the Salzburg E flat Concerto, K. 271. The other E flat Concerto, K. 449, is a member of no family; it is indeed unique among concertos.

In my young days the last of the E flat Concertos of Mozart was a favourite, its place having been taken since by the A major and the D minor. I often wish I could hear it played by one of the older pianists, for its lengthy free passages seem to demand rather the application of a perfect technique than the display of interpretative brilliance. Fifty years ago, the singer or player who appeared with orchestra at an important concert had served a longer apprenticeship than is required nowadays, albeit with a smaller syllabus and a narrower artistic outlook; control of rhythm, dynamics, phrasing, and pedalling, the smoothness and shading of scale and arpeggio passages, the fundamental things of keyboard technique—these were the first demands of a pianist; and when they were combined with the personal address of a great and sound musician, they gave more satisfaction than does the uncontrolled 'interpretation' of a Bright Young Thing. I would pay more than I could afford to hear Fanny Davies play the big E flat concerto upon a good old Broadwood or Bechstein.

The unusual amount of solo work, not to be called *bravura*, serves to mark the crispness of actual subjects as they return or are introduced. Subjects are well defined and in great number. If we gave a full diagram of the movement, we should have to label the orchestral prelude A B C D E F G, for there are seven tunes of sufficient character and identity that any two of them, were they selected for contrast, could make the total thematic material of a Schobert or Christian Bach concerto-opening. How very personal to Mozart, and not to any particular Mozart, Salzburg or Vienna, is one of these little tunes! In his G minor Piano Concerto, Dvořák actually produces a tune very like it, except that he misses the witty interval at the end; what a world of difference would be made if Mozart's last note were E flat, not F! And no other composer would have scored its repetition as in Ex. 135.

Tunes like that remove a difficulty which many musicians must feel as they look at this concerto after studying its predecessors; the extreme ease and euphony of K. 482 make one say, 'This is a longer work than K. 449 but not a greater. I would rather have the earlier and more temperamental concerto. Mozart seems in K. 482 to revert to the *galanterie* of the very first E flat Concerto, K. 271. Apparently he had not charmed or educated his audience with works like the D minor and C major Concertos.' It is possible to give several answers to this, for instance:

1. The very movement which Mozart had to repeat, and whose encore surprised Leopold, was the middle one in C minor, the least suave and *galant*.
2. The suavity and euphony of which, in some moods, we tire, is by no means typical of Mozart's age but is one facet of Mozart's creative personality, and it so happens that we know both Mozart and his age chiefly through that facet.
3. As music, we cannot but hold K. 449 to be among Mozart's most admirable works—its concentration, its operatic 'temperament', the wit of its finale—make it a rare and cutting gem. What we demand from modern music, and what we enjoy in the music which came after Mozart, flatters the standards by which we judge K. 449 and by which K. 482 is but a longer, not a greater, work.

It is as a concerto that the later work advances upon the earlier; the fact that this huge first movement, so rich in thematic as in free matter, does not flag shows a mastery of the form as consummate and as capable of diversity as is exemplified by its great predecessors. This becomes more obvious when we make a diagram in which only one letter is used wherever two tunes always hunt together:

Orchestral prelude	A	B	C	D.			
Exposition	x . . . A . . . . y . . . z . . .						
First ritornello	C	D.					
Middle section	D . . y . . . z						
Recapitulation	A	B . . . z					
Final ritornello	C	D.					

The solo not only opens with a new tune but continues with new materials throughout an exposition which is so deferential to the piano that it borrows only one theme from the prelude, and keeps that for the orchestra. When A enters, its trumpets and drums emphasize its ritornellic function and also the concertante nature of everything else in the exposition. In such an exposition the free writing needs, and has, the utmost grace and beauty.

The recapitulation, cunningly condensed as will be seen in the diagram, gives the impression of ample length and freedom, but includes, I feel, a structural mistake. The last spate of free writing is made of the same themes as the cadenza, and must have sounded particularly drawn out in days when pianists added an interesting composition by Hummel. In fact, with the cadenza, the final ritornello is too long, and it seems wise to follow the recommendation of Peters' Edition and to make the last ritornello a plain C–D; the ear does not need the whole ritornello to appreciate the general scheme.

We have no cadenza by Mozart himself, and Hummel's cadenza, though not to be used by any player with a sense of balance and structure, is excellent Hummel. In spite of the many hard things said of the old Hummel and Cramer editions of Mozart, they *may* bear more resemblance to Mozart's own practice than do chaster modern editions. They remember that the left hand should never be idle; they keep its continuo function; their figurations are well done, though we may question whether some of them should be done at all. It is unlikely, for instance, that Mozart left Ex. 136 as it stands.

2. *Second Movement, Andante*

This movement was not discussed in the chapter on variations since its form is hybrid. Four variations on a pathetic C minor theme are interspersed by two episodes, one in relative and one in tonic major. But for their position, where they seem exquisite Mozart, the episodes would be no great matter.

It was this very movement which Mozart had to repeat; the audience was a select one. The 120 subscribers had been trained in their listening, and in their hearts was that love of 'sentiment' which is one of the interesting preludial phenomena of the full romantic movement. At times this C minor piece seems to have no more emotional content than the term just used implies. It does not, to modern ears, have the same disturbingly beautiful effect as the G minor Variations of K. 456, but the same methods are used in the making of its theme— pathetic repetitions, pathetic moves to and from the relative major, pathetic sforzandi, pathetic prolongation of the last phrase. One cannot be sure that Mozart is writing other than 'detachedly' as he adopts this style a second time in a concerto; beforehand we felt the emotion to be deeply and personally felt (Exx. 137 and 138).

Nevertheless, this is a fine piece, unique in Mozart for the exquisite wind writing alone; to hear the instruments in performance is to gain a much deeper impression than by playing the score at home and imagining the instrumental effects. The solo embellishments of the theme have the same high quality as in the two previous Variation-

andantes, K. 450 and 456, and the use of what we may call 'interrupted variation form' is as splendid as in the Haydn symphonies
from which, no doubt, Mozart learnt it. This C minor movement
would be more memorable did not Mozart himself lead us to expect
rather an unusual experience in C minor middles to works in E flat;
for it is just below the level of slow movements like that to the Sinfonia Concertante.

3. *Finale, 6/8*

The first phenomenon upon which one is expected to comment
when discussing this finale has been previously observed in the finale
of K. 271, the Salzburg E flat Concerto; a long episode in gracious

serenade style breaks into the 6/8 hilarity, taking the place of the usual middle episode. Apparently this occurrence is as inevitable after the words 'in E flat' as is the demand for clarinets upon the score paper. Two short cadenzas make the necessary joins.

The Rondo is made of street tunes, the first of which is like its opposite in the B flat Concerto, K. 450, and even more like the 'won't go home till morning' spirit of the Salzburg Horn Concertos (see Exx. 139*a* and *b*). Naturally the structure is of the loosest, and rightly so; only Haydn made elaborate structure of hilarity, but not with what one could honestly call street tunes. Now there are people who call a Rondo like this one the 'weakest' movement of its concerto, and we have already seen that, when he wished, Mozart could imbue rondo with emotional power and constructive skill. When he does not decide to make the form a vehicle for these particular qualities, must the result be necessarily weak? Mozart wrote some weak and vapid rondos, and when they mar a concerto one says so; but in the instance now being examined, this string of popular tunes is more exhilarating than is the Rondo of K. 450, with its solo virtuosity and clever treatments of the main theme; and the K. 450 Rondo is no-where regarded as a poor specimen. Two qualities prevent the E flat Rondo from being justly labelled weak, as they also prevent the jolly and more conventional horn Rondo quoted at Ex. 139*a* from being so labelled.

In the first place the tunes are spontaneous, and their arrangement has a near-illusion of spontaneity. Such spontaneity is rare among highly cultured (i.e. trained) composers when they have not the opportunity to display their advanced craft. Schubert and Brahms might have made good street musicians had they not also been great symphonists; Beethoven and Wagner would not have done well in the role of Irving Berlin—an inspired artist who, I learn, played only with one finger and upon the black notes. Sir Felix Batholiver, Commissar Designate of British Music, would be not a great teacher, but a great artist, if his highly cultured and well-written occasional pieces for full orchestra and chorus had the spontaneity of a Strauss waltz. Is Mr. Berlin, then, the better for having little academic training?

It is hard to answer that question; but we suppose that Mr. Berlin's best songs derive their vitality from the fact that they are written at full strain on his creative powers and musical knowledge. If Sir Felix wrote with a *portion* of his own powers and knowledge (as indeed do certain sham folk-song manufacturers and pseudo-modal traffickers)

the result would be unpleasant unless it were a deliberate parody.
Tovey says in one of his lectures on the Integrity of Music: 'The
vulgar popular author often does not know that literature and art
contain higher thoughts than his own, and unless he is a cynical
moneymaker, the discovery of this truth would probably dry up his
inspiration from the source.' Tovey recalls the centipede whose
inspiration was paralysed by a malicious snail, who asked him which
leg he put down first, and the centipede, perspiring in the ditch considering how to crawl, is likened to the artist whose technique is not

139 (a)

Horn Concerto. K.447.

(b)

K.482.

140.

Solo

Orch.

driven into the subconscious by an access of inspiration. Mozart,
like Handel, turned out his second and third best, and people are
attracted by little tunes which have the period flavour not recognizable by Mozart's own contemporaries. Parry therefore had little
use for Mozart except as The Predecessor, and Parry's blindness has
been responsible for false assessments of Mozart's art which are still
widely accepted, since Parry's contributions to works of reference
have not yet been wholly superseded. Parry failed to recognize that
Mozart 'wrote down' a good deal more badly than Parry would have
done, but that Mozart could make money by 'writing down', whereas
Parry had the lucky position of Sir Felix. A movement, therefore,
which is a brilliant and consistent whole, which coheres as convin-
cingly as a sonata-form, and yet is as loose and as spontaneous as a

street song, must be regarded as a gem when it bears the image and not merely the superscription of a highly cultured artist like Mozart.

Secondly, however facile the movement *appears*, there are unexpected things in it, and the tunes themselves do not seem so facile if one tries a simple experiment. One knows of so many Mozartian rondo tunes which people rightly call light and trivial; but if one selects those which are vital and saucy with Mozartian wit, and if one then tries to add to their number, one is made to recognize something which pays tribute to their originality. In what dance-measure is any one of them? If one were dealing with a gigue or a siciliano, one could invent another tune for oneself, for one would be applying musical knowledge, not channelling inspiration; but Mozart's best rondo tunes are unexpected if we have not heard them before—heard *them*, I say, not other tunes. And if there are other tunes, if Mozart's best rondo tunes are the small change of *le style galant*, in what works of other composers do we find their fellows? If one had never heard Ex. 139*b*, I do not think one could invent its brother; one's attempt to do so would be as much like the genuine creature as are the pictures of elephants (with trunks sticking to their faces as on a child's plasticine elephants) seen in medieval psalters, and painted by men who had heard the elephant described but had not seen it walking. Mozart seemed aware, however, that more was required in so long a movement than the most ebullient string of melodies; he therefore indulged the unexpected in matters of procedure, though he did not draw for the purpose upon the resources of academic technique; street melodies would not bear the treatment. One instance of Mozart's trickery in this movement may serve as an example. There is a little tune of five phrases which comes just after the first strophe and its ensuing portion of brilliant solo work (Ex. 140). At the end of the whole rondo we come to the usual brave cadence with repeated chords in the tonic key. The delighted simpletons begin their applause, but the Man with the Score hisses and scowls, for the band is playing *piano* and the piano is playing *dolce*. Playing what? Not Ex. 140 exactly, but a version of it which only a Mozart could have invented; the five phrases are made into three, and the trumpets and horns play the genuine last cadences, making the tally-ho noises which are reminiscent of the 'Song for All Husbands' in *Figaro*.

CHAPTER XVI

CONCERTO IN A, K. 488

CONCERTO IN A MAJOR, K. 488. *Completed by 2 March 1786*
  1. Allegro, 4/4.
  2. Adagio (André) or Andante (Breitkopf) in F sharp minor, 6/8.
  3. Allegro assai (André) or Presto (Breitkopf), 2/4.

Orchestra: Strings, one flute, two clarinets, two bassoons, two horns.

Biographical notes

In the two and a half months since K. 482 the most important event is the performance of a small work, the one-act comedy *Der Schauspieldirektor* (usually in this country called *The Impresario*) in the orangery at Schönbrunn, for which setting it was commissioned by the emperor. No doubt during the period which brought forth the Concertos in E flat, A, and C minor, Mozart's chief thoughts and hopes were for the completion and successful launching of *Figaro*.

One of his letters mentions the A major Concerto amongst others. The letter is dated 30 September 1786 and is to Sebastian Winter, who was once the Mozarts' *friseur*, and in 1764 became valet to Prince Fürstenberg at Donaueschingen. K. 488 was among some concertos and symphonies ordered by the prince, and Mozart sends, via Winter, an account for the works, their copying and postage.

'The compositions which I keep for myself or for a small circle of music lovers and connoisseurs (who promise not to let them out of their hands) cannot possibly be known elsewhere as they are not known even in Vienna; and this is the case with the three concertos [K. 451, 459, and 488] which I have the honour of sending . . . and I must ask His Highness not to let them out of his hands. . . . There are two clarinets in the A major concerto. Should His Highness not have clarinets at his court, a competent copyist might transpose the parts into the suitable keys, in which case the first part should be played by a violin and the second by a viola.'

This passage shows that Mozart associated the clarinets with special moods and with works of special character, the usual keys being E flat or A major. In such works he evidently considered the

141.

142.

oboes obtrusive and inartistic, not merely a poor substitute for clarinets. We may regard as nonsense the suggestion that, with K. 482, Mozart thought he would 'write down' to the Vienna public by reverting to Salzburg *galanteries*. The 120 subscribers, mentioned in Leopold's letter (which I have quoted in the biographical notes to K. 482) were a trained audience who brought out the best in their performer-artist. The jolly Rondos of K. 482 and K. 488 do not pander; whether we like them or wish that the Dignity of Art had

143.

144.

145.

manifested itself in their place, they are there because Mozart wanted them there.

1. First Movement, Allegro

THE concerto begins (Ex. 141) like someone resuming a pleasant tale, not like a speaker making a dramatic announcement. Much has been made of the masterly originality which opens Beethoven's first symphony; some writers would lead us to suppose that its first audience received a violent shock because the first chord was not in tonic harmony. It is hard to see how Mozart's first chord and the quiet shift from subdominant to tonic harmony in this concerto should have been reckoned less original; the phrase seems the musical equivalent of '. . . as I was saying'. Mozart's symphonies are, at least as regards structure, a conservative series, but he introduced as many novelties to the piano concerto as Beethoven did to the symphony; conversely, beneath the very different *Stimmung* of Beethoven's first concertos there is little structural novelty. Instead, there is the tremendous forward thrust of Beethovenian texture. A strikingly original movement like the slow one in the G major Concerto vindicates Mozartian principles while transcending them.

To those who have not examined Beethoven's first movements very carefully it may seem that he introduced decidedly novel first-entries for the solo; Mozart has quite a number of novel gambits—a greater number than Beethoven because there are more concertos. What is more, they are not less original than Beethoven's. Through the very different turns of a different genius, Beethoven's first entries happen to assert their departure from type more obviously than do Mozart's. In fact, all Beethoven's novelties are more directly patent. If a listener's turn of mind is Beethovenian, he calls these novelties dramatic or bold; if he is a violent classicist and dislikes Teutonic romanticism of the period, he calls them theatrical. It is a mark of wider musical and mental experience to relish both conservatism and adventurousness in genius.

Of the great concertos, this is the sunniest, its mood being similar to that of the 'Little A major', K. 414; it is difficult to say why this work is greater than the other, if we try to do so from any one aspect—keyboard figuration, scoring, structure, &c. Despite the advance in each of these directions, artistic perfection remains perfection in the work written four years before, and, if we were to judge only by the allegro movements, we should have no right to speak of K. 488 as the greater work. One might as well ask organists which of Bach's fugues in G minor or in E minor is the more perfect. (Dangerous question as regards the G minors, since the 'Great' G minor, for all its magnificence, is too long by several bars of the last page.)

The technical feature which gives the 'sweet' flavour to this concerto, and also turns that sweetness to sentiment, is the use of suspensions over mild discords in those subjects which are most in evidence. In discussing the opening of the slow movement of the G major Concerto, K. 453, I have called attention to the power of a suspension or delayed appoggiatura, which has the same effect as has the delaying of eating while our mouths water. A chain of suspensions over chords of the sixth is a stock-in-trade of Mozart and Haydn, which genius turns to beauty like Ex. 142. The opening of the slow movement is full of the same device, using the same intervals as Elgar took for the 'Nimrod' variation (Ex. 146, places marked *a*). It is well to compare the themes here with those in the C minor Concerto, whose subject has directness and power, being without suspensions or ornaments. In that concerto, harmonic intricacies involve clashes of a major second or have the acerbity of Ex. 159, not the honeyed poise of seventh moving to sixth. The contrasts are reinforced by scoring; it is impossible to imagine the A major Concerto with the bite of oboes or without clarinets.

One should not be surprised at the difference between a concerto and its predecessor in the series; surely this should be expected. Both K. 482 and K. 491, on either side of this K. 488, have long, elaborate first movements, with much new material after the entry of the solo. In K. 488 the exposition is only four bars longer than the prelude, which announces both main subjects. This, therefore, is the single concerto in the series:

1. Which has only two main expository themes.
2. Adds no new material for the solo.
3. Repeats all preludial themes in the exposition.

In other words, this might be the one text-book concerto by Mozart; but it is not. The text-book is foiled of its one specimen capture immediately the exposition is over. From the moment of the customary shake on the dominant, K. 488, like any other K. worth discussing, becomes as unique in structure as in character. We have had expositions which do not repeat the prelude and recapitulations which do not repeat the exposition; now we have a middle section of entirely new material. The diagram is as follows:

Orchestral Prelude	A	B	C	D.
Exposition	A	B	C.	
First ritornello	B	E.		
Middle section	E	(piano variation)	F	G.
Recapitulation	A	B	C	E	Free writing.
Final ritornello	B	E	Cadenza	D.

The novelty begins in the first ritornello. In most concertos Mozart retains the last theme of the prelude to be used only as the last theme of ritornelli; as such it is often of haunting cadential beauty. The ritornello in question has no such rounding off; it does not finish at all, for when it has introduced E (Ex. 143) the piano gives it a variation and sets off with material for the middle section— the ritornello and middle section are inseparable. Of the two themes which follow, F and G, one orchestral, the other markedly pianistic, the first has the same rhythm as E (see Ex 144), but the leap of a fifth makes it useful for the wonderful interplay which occupies the second half of this middle section; Ex. 143 shows the seeds and Ex. 145 their germination.

Rumour has it that this concerto is easy, and that its cadenza seems to have been written for a pupil. Most performances one hears help to show how easily rumour spreads. Amongst the many who have sought to provide something more substantial than Mozart's own simple cadenza is a Frenchman who has published his efforts, and whose composition shows as little belief in the use of anaesthetics as does his performance. Unless one is insensitive to structure, one will not employ material in cadenza which has already been heard thrice; one will learn from Mozart's humble effort or—who knows?—play the poor thing after all.

Tovey's remarks upon this abnormally built movement are quoted:

'Thus, when the recapitulation is reached, the old themes return with complete freshness. And, what is perhaps more remarkable though less obvious, the development had none of the looseness of effect that in ordinary sonatas is apt to result from basing it mainly upon "episodes".

The episode here was a thing of absolute dramatic necessity. And after the now inevitably and rightly regular recapitulation, Mozart paradoxically vindicates his principle of making the solo refer more closely to the orchestra than to its own exposition of themes.'

2. *Second Movement, Adagio*[1] *or Andante*

Mozart's only movement in F sharp minor is one of his most emotional; from the outset, two persons seem present, both of whom are singers, and both of whom sing of the same grief from two points of view, as though one would console the other but cannot, so must share the grief. Their voices are not so far contrasted as soprano and contralto; they are about as far removed as those of the countess and Susanna. The technical vehicles of their emotion are the suspension, the vocal climax with a pause or hiatus, and the favourite Neapolitan Sixth which follows the climax as if in abandonment to grief.

The opening theme is one of the loveliest in all music. It is also

146.

---

[1] MS. in Paris Conservatoire Library, reproduced in Saint-Foix, vol. iv. All generally accessible editions have 'Andante', which word I have used loosely for all concerto slow movements.

147.

148.

the fine product of a highly complex brain, however spontaneous its
inspiration. At risk of being thought Philistine, let us inspect it very
closely (Ex. 146). There is at least one suspension in every bar,
except the first. The balance of two-plus-two bars, with which it
opens, is without formality, the two phrases marked *a* being separated
by a suspension which neatly hides the middle crack by spreading
across it. After this not-straightforward four-bar tune we have a
phrase of seven bars which will assure an inspired asymmetry. First
two bars with discord resolving upwards, echoed by two others with
discord turning downwards; then the Neapolitan Sixth, the vocal
climax, the sorrowful abandonment. When the second voice, represented by the orchestra, joins in sympathy, suspension overlaps suspension (Ex. 147). At the second entry of the solo, we have the only
writing in the whole movement which is quite unvocal, though it is
not suggested that any other part would be a whit more expressive
if taken from the piano; the soft plashing (as Purcell's weeping
nymphs termed the sound of their pathetically fallacious fountains)
is an important contribution no less in the cantabile line than in
elaborations of pure pianism.

When we reach the coda we find, used in a way impracticable for
the voice, a device by which singers showed their mastery of technics; it is wonderful how, when struck from the piano against a bare
pizzicato on the bare strings, the 'vocal leap' over intervals greater
than an octave can give so poignant an expression of dignified grief
(Exx. 148–150). In making this comment one is forced to speak of matters textual, which one would fain avoid in a book of this kind. It is
widely accepted that this coda, as it has come to us, has an incomplete
part for the piano—'a mere sketch'. One remembers no performance
at which a pianist dared to fill in the outline, and one is dissatisfied

with tentative completions by Hummel, Fuchs, Reinecke, or even Girdlestone. I feel certain that no tentative completion should interfere with the plain notes for the right hand, nor should any left hand accompaniment contain notes shorter than quavers. If Mozart did not play the passage as it stands, he may have given the left hand quiet repeated chords at each quaver, and a soloist who adopted this treatment could quote the slow movement of the G major Concerto, K. 453 for precedent, since in that lovely piece the right hand has the beautiful 'vocal leaps' in single notes. But one remembers another point, the last bars of the refrain theme which opens the slow movement of K. 491 in C minor, which many critics cannot believe to be what Mozart wrote. In discussing that point I have recorded my opinion that no other ending is acceptable, and that I have never myself felt uneasy at the passage as it stands. In this debated part of K. 488 my experience has left me not merely accepting the so-called 'outline' as it stands, but finding in its single right-hand notes against the bass pizzicato an effect of such extreme beauty as would justify the theory that it is deliberate.

I see nothing in the appearance of the Paris manuscript to put such a theory out of court but, while dealing with the subject of that manuscript, one should mention its heading of this movement by the direction Adagio. The editions all have Andante, which is in accord with the nature of this movement as musical terms are followed to-day. It may easily have been the better term in Mozart's day, since his pupils or followers approved the change in early editions, and he himself may have had the afterthought. If the Adagio of Beethoven's 'Hammerklavier' Sonata, also in F sharp minor and showing curious resemblances to the Mozart piece, had been labelled Andante, it would be better played. It is the deeply pathetic *nature*, both of the Mozart and the Beethoven piece, which makes us prefer the word 'adagio', and no doubt that is what made Mozart use the word on the autograph score. But if this word makes a soloist play the movement in a dragging manner, or with rubato, manhandling it as the Beethoven movement is usually manhandled, it is well that he sees only the 'andante' mark which follows the Breitkopf and Härtel edition of 1800, though André's edition had retained the autograph directions.

3. *Finale, Allegro assai, 2/4*

The slightness of this movement may be judged from the specimen of 'construction' given at Ex. 153, yet it is virtuosic as composition and not just pianistically. When rondo is structurally virtuosic we

judge it as music rather than as rondo. The finale of Brahms's D minor Concerto is a great movement; the 'gipsy' tunes of his B flat Concerto make a great rondo. So do the tunes of K. 488.

Its first audience had listened to two movements whose beauty prevented smiles; the second of them would have drawn tears from a stone. The rondo should therefore be light and entertaining. A digression in form of a true story is appropriate to a critical appreciation of this rondo. The publisher of a very serious and highly esteemed English composer asked him to pause before writing more symphonies and to write something 'that would get him better known with the populace'—and, of course, bring money to the publisher. I was able to hear the composer's conversation after the interview. He made some reflections on these lines: 'He cannot recognize that I have no genius for light music, and that any attempt to write it will do me no good artistically or commercially. I hold men like Edward German in the highest honour, and admit that such men are lucky in having a genius for music that is immediately and widely popular. Mozart was like that, and in modern conditions Mozart would make a fortune with the products of one side of his genius which he would lose in performances of works of the other side.' The point emphasized by these remarks is that genius is not always recognized when it lurks behind shallow materials.

There are few suspensions about these tunes. Their shallowness is evident in their unusually simple harmony and scoring. Each half begins like its other half in any of the themes, but at such speed and in such high spirits all this is desirable. It is when we get similar symmetrical and slender themes in languishing slow movements that their repetitions are tiring.

In K. 488 Mozart could have written a rondo of virtuosic structural intricacy. Fortunately he did not, though there is one spot that takes the smile off one's face (Ex. 154), not because the merriment ceases, but because one is suddenly made aware of the presence of genius. The attention demanded by genius (for reasons which the psychologist may explain) brings the involuntary respectful attention which is given to solemn art. One may do less than justice to the English and Teutonic races in supposing that they respect a work of art in direct relation to its solemnity. If we do not share that widespread mistake, we shall not regard Ex. 154 as the finest passage in the rondo; rather shall we enjoy transition writing like Exx. 151 and 152 which no composer but Mozart could spin so delicately.

Ex. 153 is one of many quotations made in this chapter which bear

witness to the fact that a chief contributor to the ebullience and
brilliance of such concertos is the regular and rapid stroke of ham-
mers. Many soloists slither through the 'mere transition passages'
like this example, using clear strokes only upon the first beat of the
bar. At the same time it is hard to blame the pianist or conductor
who unconsciously gets faster during this movement, for we all 'get
faster', rioting with the composer in the high spirits of the scales at
the end, or the extra tunes to the rondo proper, such as Exx. 152 or
153. The movement finishes like the overture to a comic opera. The
popularity of this concerto, when first played, and now, is very
understandable.

CHAPTER XVII

CONCERTO IN C MINOR, K. 491

CONCERTO IN C MINOR, K. 491. *Completed by 24 March 1786*

1. Allegro, 3/4.
2. Larghetto, in E flat major, 4/4.
3. Allegretto (variations) 4/4, last variation in 6/8.

Orchestra: Strings, one flute, two oboes, two clarinets, two bassoons, two horns, two trumpets, two drums.

Biographical notes

Since this concerto followed the A major within three weeks there are no external events to record.

THE similarity of the opening theme (Ex. 157) to that of C. P. E. Bach's Concerto in F minor (see Ex. 15 above and also the quotation here, Ex. 155) makes one wonder if Mozart knew Bach's fine work, which his own concerto resembles in spirit.

The second of Mozart's two concertos in a minor key is quite unlike the first in D minor; it is as passionate, but less stormy and more spacious. Of all classical concertos, it would be the most spacious were it not rivalled by K. 503 in C major or Beethoven's in E flat. Many musicians must find this work a touchstone in the understanding of its maker; how many of those who now acknowledge it as the summit of Mozart's art in this form were unable to grasp it at first acquaintance? Its slow movement has quite recently received the disapproval of an august pen; its finale, Mozart's finest essay in variation form, is abnormal; and he who finds the first movement not a bar too long nor a theme too diffuse may consider *se valde profecisse* in the Mozartian conception of concerto form. Study of this work from structural, psychological, or technical points of view might fill a whole book. Its orchestration alone (though, with Mozart, no one element in composition can be studied alone) should make its miniature score the obligatory possession of the impecunious student.

1. *First Movement, Allegro*

Cussedness must account for many a critical exaggeration; writers of the past referred too glibly to 'Haydn and Mozart', so a modern critic must go to the length of declaring the two men 'as utterly different in musical expression as two composers of the same epoch could possibly be'. (Since the two men differ so much in temperament and upbringing, surely the most remarkable thing about their musical expression is its frequent similarity.) This tendency to over-correction is most unjust to Mozart when it sets out to justify his ways to people who recognize one musical god and Beethoven as his prophet. Put simply, such writing seems to say: 'You folk who still live in the backwash of romantic pianism seem to find Mozart spiritually cold; but the fault is with you, who are too dull to see the turgid passions which seethe behind many a formal and tongue-tied work. Go to your scores again, especially to those in minor keys, and you will find one of the greatest of 'romantics.' Determined not to be branded dull, we go back as we are told, and find what we are told; Mozart is now a romantic; let us be the foremost in the cult. What sentiments too deep for tears lie behind these minor keys!

The first requisite of a cult is faith, not sense, nor reason; the senses are gross and reason a destroyer. The senses must·be held in check to wait on faith and fortify it. No wonder that faith is said to remove mountains; it will remove black marks from a score, reverse indications of time and expression, turn crotchets into quavers, and show the faithful just what the pontiffs want them to see. Before Mozart left Paris for the last time, his audience included the last representatives of the most conventional epoch in European history; eleven years later the Revolution ended their reign in France, but not elsewhere. To Dr. Johnson's less intelligent contemporaries, 'civilization had arrived' and its values had come to stay; to more sensitive frequenters of Mozart's 'academies', new and strangely exciting vistas were opening in the realms of thought and feeling, and Mozart's most personal expression, disturbing to the *Kapellmeister* mentality, must have thrilled the finer minds. If we are to know Mozart as he was, is, and always will be, we must trust our eyes and ears to reveal a wonder far greater than the miniature Beethoven which romantic faith wants us to create.

This wonder is one of the most sensitive products of a great age, the eighteenth century, whose scale of values was different from, though not inferior to, that which the age of Beethoven put in the

ascendant. Better Schumann's limited vision with eyes peering at
Mozart than the eye-of-faith tied to its own aesthetic reactions.
J. C. Bach rarely dared to write a concerto in a minor key; but, since
he was not one of the advanced thinkers and poets of his age, he was
not prompted to experiment with audiences which were pleased with
conventions. Mozart was bound to do so, and it is immaterial that
his use of a minor key-signature coincided with one of Constanze's

155.

156.

frequent *accouchements* or with one of her husband's frequent finan-
cial embarrassments. The C minor Concerto was not merely in
advance of its age; it is also in advance of ours. It is unique, but so
are a dozen Mozart concertos, as are a dozen Gothic cathedrals; and
there are whole passages, even whole works, in which the manifold
ranging of Mozart's expression seems to anticipate that of Beethoven.
When this occurs, as in the C major Concerto, K. 503, it is not
denied; but it occurs very, very rarely in K. 491. Nor do I see what
has been called 'a certain feverishness and strained nervousness' in
the work; if it were not impassioned, there would be no need to waste
time in its study, though it is true that none of its fellows is so consistently serious, so continually oscillating between the tenderness of
the major key and the reassertion of minor sombreness.

Despite Beethoven's admiration of this concerto—oh to have heard him play it!—the first movement shows the extreme limit to which the rich, ample, *classical* conception can be pushed. A comparison with the first movement of Beethoven's C minor Concerto is not fair to Beethoven, since we are dealing with Mozart's greatest concerto movement, and we have no right to judge the Beethoven work by Mozartian standards. What makes the Beethoven diagram look so ridiculous is the absence in it of any representation of his most personal contributions to the form, the almost kinetic development of themes which are best described by the hackneyed adjective 'pregnant' and whose type Mozart rarely conceived. The diagrams merely give the themes in their order, thus:

Beethoven

Orchestral prelude	A	B.
Exposition	A	B.

Mozart

Orchestral prelude	A	B	A	C	D.
Exposition	x	A	y	A	z	A.

To take the diagrams farther is to make the parallel the more ludicrous, but already we see something unusual, in that Mozart's exposition does not draw much upon material announced in the prelude; nor, in the full diagram, is there much ritornellic use of any theme but A; instead, we find still more new matter appearing after the exposition. The ground plan is further complicated by the fact that the first subject has two ligaments, and should be represented therefore by the letters A–a, since each is used both for ritornello or for modulatory development, either by itself or in combination with its partner (see Ex. 157). The full plan is as follows:

Orchestral prelude	A	a	B	A	C	D				100	bars.
Exposition	x	A	a	y	a	z	A	a		166	,,
First ritornello	a	E								17	,,
Middle section	x	A	a	E	E	E				80	,,
Recapitulation	A	a	z	y	B	C	Free	a		111	,,
Final ritornello	A	Cad.	D	(Coda with piano)						50	,,

Reference to the score will confirm the following points shown in the diagram:

1. The orchestral prelude is wilfully stretched out to a hundred bars, although only one of its themes (the two-part A–a) is to figure extensively in concertante sections, or in the ritornelli, one of which brings in a new theme which cannot, by definition, be ritornellic. I refer to E in the diagram.

2. The two main concertante sections are more profuse of themes (which, *pace* Tovey, can hardly be said to form groups) than are the corresponding sections of any concerto.

3. There is hardly any 'free' writing, though much interplay of contrasted themes and much development of single themes.

4. The final section is peculiar, not so much because of broken chords by the piano, in its coda, as because of the strange insertion of two bars, unrelated to any particular theme, which follow the cadenza. As Mozart's cadenza or cadenzas to this movement are not known, the mystery of the missing final shake and the new inserted bars remains unsolved. The manuscript (Royal College of Music) gives no clue.

Certain of these points call for fuller examination. Why did Mozart, even more amply than Beethoven in his C minor Prelude, spin out a hundred bars of orchestral texture for its own sake? Why this preliminary symphony with material we are not meant to bear in mind as we approach the concertante sections? Tovey has answered these questions. He says: 'The opening of the first movement . . . had been developed by Mozart on a scale that has not to this day been surpassed; with the result that the entry of the solo must, if it means anything at all, mean an event impressive because long delayed . . . and the expectation must be aroused by the music and not by the title of the work on the programme.' To its original audience, the opening of the C minor must have been highly surprising, but had there been a short and undeveloped prelude, the new solo theme (x) would have formed a little concerto or aria of its own. No surprise, and no feeling of large-scale design, could be present without the long expectation and marked contrast of the solo entry (Ex. 156). The most remarkable facet of Mozart's character seems brought out here; the strongly contrasted themes, the constant pathetic soothing after theme 'A' has scowled across the scene, would have led any other composer to force our attention upon the contrast, to indulge in the theatrical, the personal, the romantic emotions. Before such a solo entry, the romantic would end his prelude fortissimo and with accented staccato bowing, certainly with the full orchestra. How can writers still regard this work as 'feverish', or as showing, all raw and callow, a list of subjective emotions worthy of Tchaikovsky? The 'Olympian serenity' of former Mozartian legend is no more present here than it is in the 'Jupiter' Symphony, to which the phrase was applied, but the constant fascination of this movement lies in the pull between its passion, its emotional inspiration, and the classical dignity and spaciousness by which its composer knew that his feelings were heightened, not damped. Unfortunately the majority of pianists know better than Mozart how to display soulfulness and spirituality; *I had not heard a single pianist play the opening phrase with control of*

157.

158.

159.

160.

time and touch till I got the Fischer recording, which, though not to everybody's taste, does at least leave the Mozart solo opening as he wrote the piece, or as it has come to us.[1]

Mozart writes of pianists who indulge in vagaries of tempo. The following passage to his father, written from Augsburg, 23 October 1777, is typical of others: 'Everyone is amazed that I can always keep

[1] Admittedly not synonymous phrases.

strict time. What these people cannot grasp is that in *tempo rubato*, the left hand should always go on playing in strict time . . . with them the left hand always follows suit. . . .' Mozart is here talking of slow movements with the usual Alberti accompaniment for L.H., but if time must always maintain periodicity, whatever justification is there for altering the speed of three plain chords like those in the third bar of our solo entry? (See Ex. 156.) I have heard this concerto punished by each of four pianists whose fees top the list. Each chooses to play the three chords mentioned, as also the all-too-simple bars three and seven of Ex. 156, *affrettando*, not, as might be a little more excusable, *poco meno e con amore*; in other words, whatever the technical prowess of these two gentlemen and two ladies, their artistic worth is to be ranked with that of the vulgar ballad-singer, with this difference—the ballad-singer's tricks are an old and expected custom, like the ornaments put in by eighteenth-century performers, and he does not pretend to be bringing his own intelligence into a creative act; he is just earning his money. These pianist-charlatans, on the other hand, have the power to poison the weaker and younger artists who have come to regard the performances of the famous as examples for imitation.

Played with dignity, tenderness, and extreme care, and without an access of fortuitous sentimentality, the opening of this piano solo, Ex. 156, can be one of the most moving things written for the instrument; it is an expression of classical emotion at its most strained, for we must recognize how impossible the *kind* of clarity displayed after the flight of bar 1 in this extract would have been to Beethoven, who would not have left the bare fifths and fourths of the bass as they are in bars 13 and 14.

There is no sense in wasting yet more paper on a discussion of the terms 'classical' and 'romantic'; they have been misused and re-assessed often enough, and an amusing evening can be spent in discussing Stendhal's remark: 'All art is romantic in its own day', or the contrary: 'All art is one day classical.' The terms are accepted as convenient historical labels, safe enough to use without straining their antithesis in detail. It is safe enough, for instance, to compare the Fifth Symphony with the *Water Music*. Among the most happy phrases which have illuminated the antithesis is one whose author I do not know, but he has said: '*After* hearing a classical work we may say "That was well written", but *during* a romantic work we may say "This is well written".'

Mozart's C minor Concerto may move our emotions deeply in the course of its performance but excites our greatest admiration for its totality; it is for this reason one of his most classical works. It seems to show, moreover, as tremendous a care in its total fashioning as in the restrained lyricism which holds the stage at points of rest, lest the tension of A–a may make the work too impetuous. Both in the exciting developments of A–a, and of themes which echo its rhythm (Exx. 159 and 160) in the careful transition from theme to theme, in the perfect judgement of each next procedure, we are aware of quali-. ties which, though claimed by Mozart himself ('enormous time and trouble'), are not those immediately associated with his name. The qualities are best understood when we try to remember an artist who possessed them in marked degree and whose genius was therefore in marked contrast to the genius of Mozart. The poet Gray bases his reputation upon less than two thousand lines of verse, most of which was frequently revised and re-polished. Amongst the concertos of the prolific and rapidly-composing Mozart, this C minor shows none of the careless rapture ('carefree' might be a better word) of many predecessors, such as the A major Concerto written so shortly before it; and it is markedly Gray-ish in comparison with the D minor Concerto which it might be expected to resemble.

The orchestration plays a great part in this emotional conditioning, and despite the perfect suiting of themes to instruments, not one of the secondary E flat tunes is *of itself* at all arresting or abnormally 'inspired' (see Ex. 158); the inspiration lies in their fitting into the general plan, and the instrumentation of each of the four of them seems to emphasize this happy placing. Like the arias of the operatic heroine, these tender little tunes hold the stage at points of repose in the drama and, as the old phrase puts it, 'improve the moment', drawing the last ounce of sweetness from the passing emotion. Such a theme as Ex. 158 might easily be the music holding the stage at the close of an aria, though the bassoons suggest that the turbulent presence of A–a is in the wings. At the end of another of these little E flat themes, A enters upon the flute and is followed by a series of diminished-seventh and six-three chords which are characteristic of late Mozart; the tortuous modulations which come later in the same part of the concerto, and their ultimate arrival in the E flat from which they began, must have bewildered contemporary ears, and are surprising to ours.

The musician will always examine two places in Concerto form to see whether the artist has drawn beauty from necessity; one is the lead from middle section to recapitulation, wherein Mozart makes daring clashes between the soloist's scales and the chords which accompany; the other is the point at which a new turn has to be given to old material in order to reach the keys proper for recapitulation. Ex. 160, which begins the modulations towards recapitulatory C minor instead of expository E flat, is surely as lovely in its classical way as is the famous swerve to F major at a similar point in the 'Eroica' Symphony. It is this kind of writing which makes Mozart's concertos more interesting than his symphonies.

In no other concerto does Mozart use so large an orchestra. A pair of beloved clarinets joins bassoons, oboes, and flute, and helps to make interplay of solo and orchestra attain a virtuosity unparalleled in the history of concerto form. The single flute here and elsewhere in these scores needs explanation since, although the transverse flute was well established by the time with which we are dealing, even Mozart is obviously set to some pains to make it plainly heard, and it shows somewhat pedantic fidelity to the score to let the second flute go for a cigarette in the band room. In his book, *The Orchestra in the Eighteenth Century*,[1] Adam Carse quotes Quantz's treatise on flute playing, in which the flute is regarded 'as a solo instrument in concerto work rather than for ripieno parts'. The smaller orchestras of the eighteenth century maintained two flutes *or* oboes, as well as the usual pairs of horns and bassoons. Oboes were the normal treble wood-wind instruments. Carse writes: 'It was only quite late in the century that the flute began to occupy an equal footing with the oboe. Up to then . . . they were not normally employed in the same movement or at the same time.' A letter of Leopold Mozart is quoted informing his son that at the Milan opera, if a score had no flute parts, the two flutes made up the oboes to four. It is plain from scores (or rather from parts, since in earlier times the clavecinist's part is the nearest approach to a score) that oboists were expected at any moment to become flautists; frequently flutes are needed just for a middle movement. Only in the larger bands were there regular flautists as well as the oboists. So perfect, however, is Mozart's writing for conventional limitations that the writing of a second, independent flute part seems impossible for the same concerto. So also must we go to Mozart to find trumpets and horns, now in octaves, now in unison, and, with the drums, used for subtler purposes than the addition of noise.

The paragraph I have to add now has no more value than any other expression of a personal opinion. The movement shows the greatest

[1] Heffer, Cambridge.

lengths to which the Mozartian, classical conception of concerto form can be complicated. The personal opinion I want to add is that, judged absolutely, this older conception bears the complication far better than does the later form. If we consider any great example of romantic symphony, which takes its architecture from rhythmic imitation of one short pregnant motive and the lyrical contrast of a very different type of theme—say, for instance, the first movement of Beethoven's C minor Symphony—and then try to conceive its bearing partnership with a solo keyboard instrument which introduces no other important themes, we must recognize that the greatest masters of musical form must have had great difficulty in obtaining a satisfactory structural result. Virtuosity on the part of the soloist is the one element which can prevent a sense of repetition or superfluity of materials. The nineteenth century was the glorious epoch of pianistic virtuosity, and now that epoch has passed, the two-subject, text-book concerto has passed with it. The concerto is dead, as Lizst and Chopin knew it. That kind of virtuosity can go no farther, and if young composers want to write a live concerto, they had better tackle the structural problem afresh, not omitting to discover for themselves the *raison d'être* of every point in the Mozartian procedure.

2. *Second Movement, Larghetto*

All here is in simple relief to the huge structure just passed. Here also is simple boredom if we have to endure a charlatan pianist who insists upon *molto adagio e molto rubato* for the main tune, and a furious gallop for the contrasting sections which, for all their froth, are shallow little brooks which seem as nothing (but mud) if their contents are made to flow away too fast. Good recordings, playing the movement in strict time, as Mozart himself declared he played his works, give one no wish to move the discs impatiently round so as to bring the fascinating finale more quickly to the ears.
The plan is as follows:

E flat
{ A solo, repeated by orchestra.
B solo with accompaniment.
A solo, orchestra accompanying alternate bars.

C minor
{ C flute, oboes, and bassoons.
C variation by piano, with accompaniment of strings.
D wood-wind, as before.
D variation as before.

| E flat | A, as at end of first section. |

A flat
- E clarinets, horns, bassoons, and flute.
- E variation by piano, with string accompaniment.
- F wood-wind, as E before.
- F variation as before.

E flat
- A solo with wind accompaniment.
- B solo with strings accompaniment.
- A solo with wind accompaniment.

Coda. New but imitative material for solo and all sections of the orchestra. No trumpets or drums.

Put more simply, this A, B, A, C, A movement is a series of refrains and variations of episodes brought off almost entirely by the scoring. It is good to read that Girdlestone, whose impatience with charlatans never transgresses politeness, gives some space to cautions against the abominable practice of taking 'A' at one speed and the sections between its returns at another.

A great deal has been said about the fourth bar of that refrain tune (Ex. 161). Ernest Newman, inveighing against Mozart idolaters in a way which is periodically useful, points to this cadence as pathetic, and Tovey writes:

'at first sight it seems hard to realise that the naivety of the fourth bar can be intentional. Yet Mozart must have thoroughly impressed upon his young pupil Hummel that its whole point was its utter simplicity. . . . Hummel published an arrangement of eight of Mozart's greatest concertos, in which he re-wrote almost every bar of the pianoforte passages and brought them up to date. Yet he did not dare to touch this bar, until at its fifth and last appearance he added one little turn.'

One does not join the ranks of those who take a printed page as sacrosanct when one accepts this fourth bar. It is surprising, but not ridiculously so, *if played in strict time*. It seems to put an amusing and salacious check on the lyricism. It is a personal matter whether the effect is amusing or merely peculiar, but the surest way by which to come over on to Mozart's side is to try some other ending to the tune which one supposes to be more consistent with the rest of the sentence—as the present writer has done at Ex. 161.

Only one other device could have given the right degree of the surprise Mozart sought, namely, the slipping in of an extra bar, as Mozart sometimes did. The vaudeville at the end of *The Seraglio* is an example. There must be many readers, however, who would never have questioned Mozart's ending had nobody mentioned it.

3. *Finale, Allegretto (variations)*

This is both Mozart's finest essay in variation form and also his best concerto finale. It has already been discussed in the chapter on variation forms; it remains to speak of it as a finale.

It is true brother to its fellow movements of K. 491 in the virtuosic interplay of solo and orchestra, and in the important share of that

interplay allotted to the wind. Mozart's attitude to the wind instruments, without injuring the rest of the orchestral balance, treated them when strings were present with as much affection as when they were alone in a serenade. The wind scoring of later composers has various points of interest, but not one of them so respects the individual character of instruments while using them in a full orchestra. With Mozart's death, this kind of wind writing disappeared, never to return.

When we notice the lengths of music which keep to C minor, and the few passages in which trumpets and drums are used in any strength beyond piano, we cannot but recognize the astounding variety of colours which Mozart suffuses upon his dark background. There is very little writing for unaccompanied solo, and when it does occur it is no more for its own sake than for the sake of the equal length of wind writing which balances it to make the 'double variation'. To its close, this remains the most *concertante* of the concertos, and its finish in C minor, rather than in the relative major found at the end of the D minor Concerto, proclaims a classical pose to the last.

There are eight variations upon the theme whose simplicity all generations have called sublime. That theme has been partly quoted at Ex. 21c, but its opening should be inspected in score to observe both Mozart's preoccupation with sombre colours and also the range of tone.

The double variation method begins at the third presentation. Exx. 162 and 163 show the brilliance of some of the juxtapositions of texture made by this method. From these antitheses it is tempting to quote at great length, for both these and the crowning final variation were born of shrewd practical thinking together with full inspiration. For the second time Mozart asked a Viennese audience of the 1780's to hear a concerto in a minor key, full of complexities and tone colours not hitherto associated with this fashionable form of concert piece. The lyrical slow movements were acceptable, since the access of sentiment had been prepared by other slow movements. In the first concerto using a minor key, the rondo with perky tunes ended in a major key with trumpets and drums, ensuring some success. The C minor work, though written for its composer's artistic satisfaction and yielding nowhere to any but his highest ideals, gives a tune and variations that must have been as immediately popular as the sets on popular airs written to make money. Schoolboys ask for records of this movement.

Whatever value we put upon any single movement from the Mozart concertos, we shall find no work greater *as a concerto* than this K. 491, for Mozart never wrote a work whose parts were so surely those of 'one stupendous whole'.

CHAPTER XVIII

CONCERTO IN C, K. 503

CONCERTO IN C MAJOR, K. 503. *Completed by 4 December 1786*
1. Allegro maestoso, 4/4.
2. Andante, in F major, 3/4.
3. Allegretto, 2/4.

Orchestra: Strings, one flute, two oboes, two bassoons, two horns, two
  trumpets, two drums.

Biographical notes

Each concert season since Mozart's removal to Vienna brought its
concertos; K. 503 is the twelfth of the mature series. It is also a kind
of summit among the fourteen, for though they show no decline in
mastery, with the exceptional poor movement which, unfortunately,
may crop up anywhere with Mozart, they are less ambitious than
K. 503; but the chief reason for this view is that, after K. 503, concertos were no longer composed steadily for the winter concerts. The
year 1786 had seen the birth of three concertos, as had its predecessor.
From K. 503 to the 'Coronation' D major Concerto, written in a style
which would show its 'occasional' purpose did we not know of it from
external evidence, there is an interval of a year and a quarter, and
from the D major to the last concerto, in B flat, the interval is of three
years. Thus K. 503 marks the end of Mozart's period of 'stardom'
as Vienna's performer-composer. It may be said that he had written
enough concertos to keep the repertory well varied, that at least
fifteen were delightful works, and the early ones would have interested
contemporary audiences more than they do us. Mozart was not an
artist to rest on his oars for long. Had he still been very active as a
virtuoso-concertist, he would have gone on writing for his performances. Either he felt he had conquered all that world, and was
temporarily without interest in it, or his heart was set on the theatre
to the exclusion of other interests; or else his popularity was waning.
The last suggestion is to be doubted if we ask the question: 'In whose
favour?' Moreover we do not yet read of any begging letters to
Puchberg.

Although only the first movement of K. 503 is the equal of the
corresponding movement in K. 491, it does make one feel that it is

deliberately complementary to its great predecessor in C minor of the previous season. What of importance happened between the March and the December of 1786? May saw the triumph of *Figaro*,

164.

165.

166.

though the prolongation of the triumph hardly augmented the lump sum of money paid for its original production. The summer, as usual, brought beautiful chamber works, including the E flat Piano Quartet, the D major String Quartet (K. 499), several trios, and the glorious duet-sonata in F, which has the dimensions and drive of an unscored symphony. A son was born to him in October and died in November. The C major Concerto is dated 4 December and the

D major 'Prague' Symphony 6 December! No doubt Mozart looked forward to his visit to Prague early in the next year, for the Bohemian capital liked him and he liked it.

167.

168.

1. First Movement, Allegro maestoso

THIS is Mozart's 'Emperor' Concerto, and had its second and third movements been as fine as its first, the whole work would have been a greater example of Mozart as a concertist than the so-called 'Emperor' Concerto is of Beethoven. No piece from Mozart's pen is more majestic than the first movement of K. 503, not even that of the 'Jupiter' Symphony, nor all the pomps and vanities of the Salzburg masses. It is the work chosen by Tovey to illustrate the spirit and structure of the classical concerto.

Tovey is anxious to show the difference between the tonal adventures, as well as the textures, proper to a symphonic opening and the very different procedures in this opening tutti; he therefore touches but lightly upon other features of this one movement, but he bids the reader note the compression and rearrangement of material in the reprise section, and the virtuosic interplay of soloist and orchestra. Tovey's flattery of the student is humiliating, but, for a more penetrating analysis than will be found here, he is referred to *Essays in Musical Analysis*, vol. iii, especially to the chapter entitled 'The Classical Concerto'.

Neither the brave scoring nor the regal rhythms could make this movement what it is; the breadth comes from the economy, which term is not the antonym of 'wealth'. In their infancy, symphony and concerto remembered their slight origins; they were born along with overture, suite, cassation, and divertimento; but once natural selection had gone far enough, once Haydn and Mozart had nurtured them, those composers who could not write in 'great swarths' had their pomposities exposed. To puff lyrical scraps with laboured developments and grave introductions was to waste pleasant materials upon ephemeral works. To survive as concertist or symphonist after 1791, a composer had to be master of a broad texture analogous to blank verse—something that did not wax lyrical or become incandescent too quickly. In concerto form the invention and nurture of the right textures was solely Mozart's work. After Beethoven, the decadence began, and therefore this C major movement of Mozart invites comparison with Beethoven's concertos, as also does Mozart's one other fine concerto to come—that in B flat, K. 595.

Now in K. 595, though there is not the slightest thematic resemblance to Beethoven, there is considerable anticipation of his structural economy; in the C major Concerto of Mozart there are, on the other hand, one or two extraordinarily Beethovenian themes, of which Ex. 168 is one; by dipping up a second example (of several possible choices) we even find modulations and keyboard figures likely to be found in a Beethoven concerto, e.g. Ex. 164. This has not been noticeable in any previous concerto. But in referring to this work as Mozart's 'Emperor', that is to say, as a work no less ambitious and profound than Beethoven's E flat Concerto, one has none of these similarities of detail in mind, for the C major of Mozart is utterly unlike any Beethoven work in its wealth and number of themes and textures. It remains processional.

The breadth of any Beethoven movement in the concertos comes from Beethoven's *kind* of economy, the ubiquity of one motive and its rhythm, such as we find in no Mozartian concerto except K. 459 in F; the principal germ of a Beethoven concerto is simultaneously main expository theme and main ritornello. The concerto is crossed with the Beethovenian symphonic conception. Recognizing that the two ideals could not coexist in one work, Beethoven decided not to begin the disintegration of concerto; for the brilliant narration and elucidation of his repentance, see Tovey on the Beethoven C major and C minor Concertos. One sentence of Tovey runs: 'In all three concertos [Beethoven's first three] the nature of the opening tutti is radically misconceived.'

We should therefore examine the opening tutti of K. 503 and see how it imparts a Beethovenian breadth to the whole movement while allowing room for such engaging little tunes as Ex. 165. The paragraphs of this tremendous prelude are as follows:

1. Forte. Six majestic bars of tonic harmony and six of dominant, each with the tailpiece that will germinate if necessary.
2. Piano. A texture of clear yet easy counterpoint, astounding to examine, easy to hear, impossible from any but one composer. This is the kind of writing I compared with blank verse, for it advances the movement and maintains interest without using crescendo. We cannot think that anything could be added to it, yet Ex. 167 shows what happens when it becomes ritornellic and has the added keyboard part.
3. Forte. An outburst of sequential scale passages, above and below the 'point' of the preceding counterpoint.
4. Piano. The first change from tonic major. A paragraph beginning in C minor and moving back to tonic major. Ex. 168 shows the theme whose three-quaver rhythm is important structurally, since it has kinship with the two preceding paragraphs. See also the use of this rhythm in Exx. 167 and 169.
5. Forte. The cadential paragraph. First fanfares and Hallelujahs, then the characteristically Mozartian delaying of the end, which finally settles on the 'point' of para. 2.

The size and interconnexion of these paragraphs rival Beethoven and transcend him in this form, for every paragraph is ritornellic, even the regal first. What would any nineteenth-century composer have done, if put into the examination room with this tutti and told to proceed to write a piano concerto? If he had shown the taste not to make the piano enter in Tchaikovskian style with a series of C major chords imitating the opening, he would probably have broken the chords, as in Beethoven's E flat Concerto, or used a free, cadenza tempo. But in order that his opening shall be fully ritornellic, Mozart devises one of his most simple and beautiful solo entries, Ex. 166. The strings entice the piano twice; a third time they begin, but are satisfied that the solo is off, getting faster and more brilliant until, at the first climax, down comes the first C major chord of the tutti. The rests in the opening paragraph, which at first seemed designed to give pomp, now seem as windows specially designed to let the solo glitter through the orchestra.

The nature of the *bravura* passages, of which this entry is one, calls for remark. The appellation 'free writing' is inept. However brilliant and accompanied, the solo part is limited and functional. Mozart left no cadenza and it is not needed; a scale and a trilled cadence are enough in so spacious and compact a piece, which yet has room in its splendid walls for a witty little march, heard in the counterpoint of Ex. 169.

2. *Second Movement, Andante*

The andante is not immediately attractive; some may find it baffling at first hearing, but not at third hearing. It is actually a very fine movement which we may liken in its effect to the slow movement of the 'Jupiter' Symphony. At first hearing of the andante from the symphony, we do not retain in our memories any big flowing themes, but we do remember some little decorative figures which turn up at various places, especially a certain cadential phrase. We have precisely the same experience with the andante of K. 503.

The reason comes from the wide rhythmic diversity of the various themes, which are not so much themes as thematic groups. Thus the opening bar has three plain crotchets giving the expectation of a broad flowing movement; and such it is, but not made from lengthy flowing sections, each marked off cadentially; within some dozen bars of the opening we find in the forefront not crotchets, but figures including demisemiquavers despite the broad undertow.

Let it be understood that the 'first hearing' is no more a disappointment than is the first hearing of the andante of the C major Symphony; the only person to be a little disappointed is the student trying to

score-read at the piano, and his difficulty is what commends the
movement to the listener, namely, that the chief interest of this

169.

andante is in its instrumentation. On no page of the score have the
strings more notes than they have rests; they give colour, rhythm,
staccato pointings for the solo or wind, but rarely a solid background
for any length of time. Once the soloist has begun, every other player
becomes a meticulous rest-counter and ornament-phraser.

Therefore, of several movements in the Mozart concertos, this one makes a fine test for the conductor, who must know his work very well if he is not to lose his head. The opening crotchets must not be dragged, yet the demisemiquavers in the offing must not be rushed; the flow must be maintained and the players made to feel the piece as a whole, though their eyes are sharply upon their parts. There is no room for vagaries of tempo, which are allowable in the C major Symphony provided nobody is made aware of them.

The form of this andante is binary sonata, that is to say, it has a small transitional section instead of a development section. The orchestral prelude suggests the more common aria form, and that is another reason for our first bafflement. We get neither the plain binary-sonata of the C major Symphony nor the aria form usual in Mozart's concertos. Mozart rarely used sonata form for his concerto andantes. An exception is that of the F major Concerto, which is not andante, and which passes in lengthy sections, whereas the C major does not. It seems to be an assembly of little curves and quirks which do not detract from the dignified slow fluidity, for the piece is neither temperamental, nervous, nor passionate. It is plainly meant to be a fit successor to the regal first movement; it therefore maintains breadth with a certain reserve.

3. *Finale, Allegretto*

This movement, too, does not commend itself to everybody at its first meeting. Mozart wishes to be playful, ebullient, as in other rondos to concertos in a major key; but he disciplines these inclinations to make the finale in keeping with the rest of the concerto, and unbuttons himself with a staidness which is unexpected from him.

At any point in the texture we may find good Mozart, and the rondo is magnificently scored, though we find no trumpets and drums except at the beginning and ending. But we may well wonder why, wishing to make a finale worthy of the other movements, Mozart did not write in the style of the F major finale to K. 459, with its fine contrapuntal paragraphs; for where is he as anxious as in this C major Concerto to preserve this continuity of mood? Not in other C major works—not in the thrush-like tunes of the C major Quintet Finale, not in the tally-ho gallop of the K. 338 symphony which begins with the most majestic trumpetings of any, nor in the 'Linz' Symphony, nor in the 'Jupiter', nor in any of the previous C major Concertos.

We have here a rondo which may not be played much faster than the gavotte speed which its opening (Ex. 170) suggests, unless we ruin the detail. If this fact does not convince us of Mozart's intention

170.

171 (a)

(b)

(c)

of unusual breadth, we have the pedal points, not found in any other rondo. The first one comes after the opening strophe, and very fine it is, though it leads to a rather vapid little second tune. Indeed the best music of this rondo is in its transitions rather than in thematic material which has breadth but little fire. One pedal-point transition leading to the reprise section lasts for twenty-two bars on the dominant bass, thus being the longest use of the device one can remember in Mozart. Ex. 171 shows the passage, and also illustrates the use of conventional figuration to build up a keyboard paragraph more in the style of J. S. Bach than of Mozart's generation.

CHAPTER XIX

CONCERTO IN D (THE 'CORONATION'), K. 537

CONCERTO IN D MAJOR (the 'CORONATION' CONCERTO), K. 537. *Completed by 24 February 1788*

1. Allegro, 4/4.
2. Larghetto, A major, 4/4.
3. Allegretto, 2/4.

Orchestra: Strings, one flute, two oboes, two bassoons, two horns, two trumpets, two drums.

Biographical notes

Letter from Mozart, at Frankfort-on-the-Main, to his wife, 8 October 1790:

'All this talk about the imperial cities is mere chatter. True, I am famous, admired and popular here; on the other hand, the people of Frankfort are even more stingy than the Viennese.' Joseph II died, and was succeeded in February 1790 by Leopold II, whose coronation is associated with a concerto written two years previously. Prof. Blume writes:

'Whether it is entitled to its name "Coronation Concerto" is uncertain. For the coronation, which took place in October 1790, Salieri and Umlauf had been sent as conductors, with 15 chamber musicians of the Wiener Hofkapelle. Mozart, who had been passed over, followed of his own accord but was not heard at the official festivities; after their termination he arranged an academy on the 15th October which failed to bring the desired success.'

The customary title has come down from André, though we do not know from Mozart's own letters that K. 537 was one of the concertos performed during the Frankfort visit. Nottebohm says that more than one concerto was played at Mozart's concert, and mentions K. 459 in F. We do know, however, from another of Mozart's letters, that he played K. 537 in Dresden on 14 April 1789.

The D major Concerto has the nature of an occasional piece written for a fashionable audience rather than for the band of Viennese subscribers who had followed Mozart's development as far as the C major

and C minor Concertos of 1786. But for the themes and developments, the Mozartian first movement (at maximum length and wealth

172.

173.

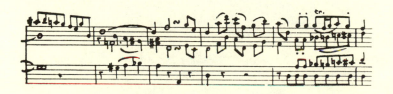

174.

of material), the Mozartian chromatics, the surprise changes of key
and mood in both first and last movements, the work seems a reversion to the *galanterie* of J. C. Bach himself.

The concerto must be regarded as an isolated phenomenon, not as a member of the progressing series, which finishes with K. 503. Mozart's wonderful last years were not in tune with the concerto

175.

176.

177.

178.

form. Two fine Quintets, the C major and G minor, and *Don Giovanni*, which are the most notable things from Mozart's pen between K. 503 and this D major work, show the expression of hitherto unexposed thoughts, and are to be regarded as among the best creations of Mozart's last period. The begging letters to Michael Puchberg, Mozart's masonic 'brother', date from the summer of 1789.

1. First Movement, Allegro

CRITICS have done less than justice to the first movement of this work; had it been shorter and had there been more interesting interplay between solo and orchestra and less mere busy-ness of the right hand alone, the tunes and the many gracious turns of phrase would have made it worthy of a place with some of the best Salzburg or early Vienna concertos. The pity is that, when a great artist reverts to a less advanced technique than he would use for his own artistic satisfaction, he does not produce as great a work of art as he does with the same technique in his early days when he drives it with all his powers. *Lohengrin* and *The Flying Dutchman* are not less vital than *Tristan* or *Meistersinger*; but imagine Wagner writing, late in life, a work which should not go beyond the vocabulary of Weber or Meyerbeer!

I once heard a fine performance of this D major Concerto in a city church, with strings alone supporting the solo. Though the organist put in a few outstanding wind passages, he told me they were unnecessary and that the score needed no arranging. This is remarkable considering that the score includes brass and drums. Yet for lengthy passages only strings are in use, and the texture at any part of the concerto is very like that in Mozart's quartets and quintets, as Exx. 172 and 173 alone show. (The last part of Ex. 173 recalls a link in the E flat Symphony, Ex. 174.)

Since Mozart's scoring is distinguished from that of others by its being so highly integral with the general conception, it can hardly be doubted that this concerto was originally written for strings and harpsichord, but that additional wind was needed for the coronation concert two years afterwards. Against this theory it has been objected that D major is one of Mozart's trumpet-and-drum keys.

The thirds and sixths of the prelude are those of Mozart's Salzburg days (see Exx. 175 and 176) even to the beautiful if commonplace cadence to Ex. 175. There is a reversion to the early concertos in many ways. For the first time since Mozart's maturity, the solo makes no thematic departures of its own after the prelude has finished. The middle section, so often the most interesting part of a first movement, is here a matter of brilliant scales and modulations. But much of the writing is by no means perfunctory. Ex. 177, for instance, is worthy of a better concerto, and the cadenza is one of the best.

There is some discrepancy between the material and the size of the movement. Mozart is about to conclude his solo exposition with the usual shake, but the music is prolonged, shifting away from A major, only to get back there like the Noble Duke of York's men. Such lengthening favours the theory that this concerto is the revision of a chamber concerto, and has been padded out to concert dimensions like the sonatas of J. C. Bach used by young Mozart.

2. *Second Movement, Larghetto*

Here is tune *et praeterea nihil*. It is a pleasant little tune, but when a pianist is administering rubato and we come to the ninth repetition we wish we had the end seats. As for what is served when the tune is not in evidence, one can only regret that Mozart stooped so low (Ex. 178).

3. *Third Movement, Allegro*

Here the trivial materials are somewhat deceptive, for should impatience drive one from the concert room one would miss some good Mozart. With a different tonal scheme, the piece would resemble first-movement form, for there is considerable compression of normal rondo form.

In Victorian times this concerto was a favourite, though the D minor became its rival. Was it the quotable portions that were enjoyed, or the conventional, euphonious brilliance in which they are embedded? One fears the latter, for that is why the concerto was written—or rather revised.

CHAPTER XX

CONCERTO IN B FLAT, K. 595

CONCERTO IN B FLAT, K. 595. *Finished by 5 January 1791*

1. Allegro, 4/4.
2. Larghetto, 4/4, in E flat.
3. Allegro, 6/8.

Orchestra: Strings, one flute, two oboes, two bassoons, two horns.

Biographical notes

This concerto is the first work whose completion dates from the year of its composer's death; in 1791 it occupies a similar position to that of the D major Concerto in 1788. Mozart's chief works during his last years are as follows:

1788. D major Concerto, the three great Symphonies, E flat, G minor, and C, waltzes and other dances for the imperial court to which he was now chamber musician, orchestrations of Handel's oratorios for Van Swieten.

1789. Early part of the year—very little. Visits to towns of north and central Germany, his first tour for many years. Beginning of quartets for the King of Prussia, clarinet quintet, work on *Così fan tutte*.

1790. Production of *Così*, 'Prussian' Quartets, concert at Frankfort which nicknames the D major Concerto of 1788, D major String Quintet, Adagio and Allegro for mechanical organ (a major work, incidentally).

1791. B flat Concerto, E flat String Quintet, 'Ave verum corpus', work on *The Magic Flute*, *The Clemency of Titus*, produced at Prague in September as part of the same coronation festivities which brought the performance of the D major Concerto, the *Requiem*.

No correspondence reveals the occasion, if any, for which the B flat Concerto was written; the small orchestra and a certain reserve about all its music suggest an intimate circle rather than the formal public concert which named the 'Coronation' Concerto. The Larghetto, whether we like or dislike it, has the unusual intimacy of a 'farewell to the piano' of Victorian memory. Girdlestone speaks of the 'vesperal' atmosphere of certain parts of the B flat Concerto and Blom calls it 'a truly valedictory work'.

There is no need here to detail once more the material and spiritual worries of Mozart's last three years. The lulls and spurts of creative

activity implied by the list of compositions are explained in standard
biographies, which show the composer's motives for touring after so
long a stay in Vienna. Of particular interest to us, and particular
delight to Mozart, was his visit to Leipzig, where he asked for copies
of Bach's vocal works and played upon Bach's organ in the Thomas-
kirche to the admiration of those who remembered the great cantor.
The writing in Mozart's Adagio and Allegro for mechanical organ, a
work now played as piano duet,[1] is worthy of one who played at
St. Thomas's.

1. *First Movement, Allegro*

THE reader is asked to pardon my narration of personal reactions to
this concerto upon two occasions. I first heard it at the age of eighteen, and, having already known three or four of the great concertos
of 1784-6, I was excited to see upon the programme note that I was
about to hear 'Mozart's last concerto'. During the performance my
heart sank; had the programme made a mistake? I knew K. 450 in
B flat, but surely this work was the other B flat, for there was a Salzburg B flat. (A little beauty, too, though I did not then know
it.) I heard the work again more than ten years later, performed
by the same group of people, yet in spite of their efforts I could
receive and enjoy the little of Mozart which was allowed to perco-
late through their performance. As I come to the work since then,
I know it and feel it to be full of gracious wisdom of a man reaching
his autumn, instead of the bare half of three-score-and-ten years
which was allotted to Mozart, and I wonder at my own previous
dullness with regard to the work.

Youth is fascinated by external complexities; the young organist
will plough through dull and bright Bach, the young pianist through
intricate and sterile studies, and it is a student of precocious advancement who is not at first disappointed with, say, the 'plain chords' in
Palestrina or the 'simplicity' of Brahms's slow movements, e.g. that to
the Third Symphony. The sort of thing admired before taste is fully
formed and the emotions are fully grown is the so-called counterpoint of the *Meistersinger* prelude.

Economy and reticence are appreciated after one's early apprenticeship in music, but in the B flat Concerto Mozart is very far from
simple; it is no revision of a childhood work, and he never reached
his second childhood. To appreciate the reticence and the power

---

[1] There are two works now called 'Fantasia in F minor', originally for mechanical
organ but now issued for piano duet. The work referred to is not the piece popular
with organ recitalists.

thereby gained, one should come to it, as does the writer, after studying the previous D major. There, one had a chamber concerto without
real intimacy, a work made externally complex for display purposes;

179.

180.

181.

182.

K. 595, on the other hand, is both complex and ambitious, but with
an economy and restraint that make it seem confidential between
composer and listener.

The opening, Ex. 179, shows Mozart's mature thinking in conventional language. The bar's accompaniment 'till ready' gives

breadth, as do the divided violas using the device before the opening of the G minor Symphony. The wood-wind ejaculation, though witty, makes for transition, for homogeneity, whatever materials follow it; it uses the notes of the common chord as did the fiddles at the opening tune, returning by plain conjunct movement. The blandness, the technical simplicity, is all that I saw as a youth. If unsuspicious or not grown musically, we see only a reed shaken with the wind; later we come to see a great prophet—which is dangerous.

Mozart and Beethoven might have been rivals, but they would have remained utterly disparate as artists had Mozart lived to a ripe old age. There happen to be curious and quite accidental likenesses to Beethoven in the last two great concertos (for we miss out the D major as not a great concerto). Mozart did not seek the same total ideal as Beethoven.

The first movement of the C major Concerto used one or two Beethovenian phrases; it was without introspection, not very urbane, and consequently Beethovenian in its heroic masculinity. But it was superior *as concerto* to anything written by Beethoven or any other composer, since it had not the slightest structural resemblance to symphony or to the Beethoven concertos, and if it could be said that this study has a central theme, that theme is the insistence that in concerto structural matters profoundly affect the musical character of the whole. That is not putting the cart before the horse.

The B flat Concerto, on the other hand, has hardly a theme or portion of a theme that makes anybody mention Beethoven (unless it be the fragment quoted at Ex. 180); unlike the C major it *is* urbane, it *is* introspective in places; it is highly Mozartian as regards materials. But the analyst sees the shape of things to come. In other words, certain structural points anticipate Beethovenian concerto, but are they not just the speciality of this concerto? Suppose Mozart had written another ten, would they have followed in this direction? The question is hard to answer, because of the gap in time which separates this concerto from the previous ones, and because the symphonies and other works give the answer 'no'. We may therefore tabulate the points which are noticeably Beethovenian in this structural development:

1. Despite the Mozartian procession of themes, there is abnormal economy.

2. Though the prelude states ritornellic materials, only one expository theme is new.

3. The only section to make a new departure in materials is the first so-called ritornello which begins with Ex. 181—which has not been heard before.

4. Ritornellic principles seem to have given way to a desire to germinate all concertante sections from first, preludial subjects.

Some of this, especially (4) was noticeable in the F major Concerto, whose first movement (and last for that matter) is close-knit in the Beethovenian sense, and in its chief 'Knitting subject', almost Beethovenian in language. Here in the last concerto is no trace of that language, but there are the methods. Let one example show it. In truly Beethovenian manner, the first ritornello is dramatically shortened before it has reached the cadence in the dominant key; but Beethoven would certainly not have used the modulation seen in Exx. 182 or 184, nor would his development section have used the whole fluid themes, altering them as Mozart does (see Exx. 182, 183, and 184). Instead he would probably have made great play with one little motive, such as the wood-wind extension of the opening tune.

While no theme is brilliantly quotable, as are themes in the 1784–6 concertos, tunes that are little at first acquaintance become emotional in their extension of development, and details like the opening 'accompanimental bar', or the octaves in Ex. 185, which seem trifling on score paper, are most beautiful in performance. In the perfect finish of sections, even when they are dramatically interrupted, we see that this concerto was a labour of love. Moreover, like nearly every previous concerto which is deeply moving as well as admirable, the texture it uses belongs to the kingdom of opera. Had not Ex. 182 been interrupted for a structural reason, it would have passed on to the music seen in Ex. 186, which is not unlike certain music of *Don Giovanni*.

2. *Second Movement, Larghetto (Breitkopf and Härtel edn. 'Andante')*

As this movement is in rondo form, we must hear the phrase quoted in Ex. 187, or at least its first two bars, eight times, and for me that is four times too often. The music is no doubt sincere, though unusual, and the expression of one mood has as much right in music as the expression of another. If we like the soulfulness of Chopin we must accept the soulfulness of Mozart—on one condition, that space and materials are commensurate with the importance of the expression. There is a difference between the size and medium of a Chopin prelude and that of a concerto movement, and I feel that in this piece, as in the Andantes of K. 451, K. 466, and this K. 595, we do not get the concerto's worth of music and Mozart; we get the

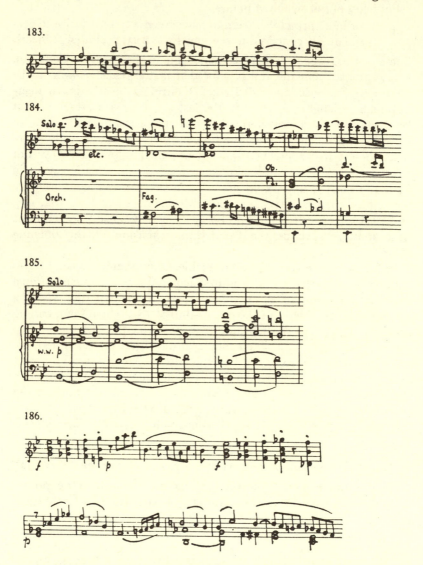

183.

184.

185.

186.

same soulful refrain several times over with by no means first-rate Mozart between its recurrences—unless you regard Ex. 188 as first-rate. It may be very distinctively Mozart, but it is surely too facile after such a first movement. Its simplicity is very different from the simplicity of restraint which we saw in the first movement, or the simplicity of wit which is to come.

We must guard against the criticism that such a tune as Ex. 188 is 'the small change of Mozart's day'. The regrettable truth is that it is unmistakably Mozart, and pianists try to find in it a grand opportunity for didactic performance. One gentleman in particular shows us poor, blind gropers what *he* sees in Mozart's little by-blows. Players who cannot command his technique or artistry, but who take it upon themselves to instruct us, in open defiance of

Mozart's views upon the use of rubato and the playing of slow movements *molto adagio*, are guilty of a complacency and arrogance that would be more obvious in any other art than music.

3. *Third Movement, Allegro*

As in the first movement, Mozart shows new economical powers in his most prolix form by germinating a great deal of movement from the main theme. Let romancers find that theme anything but vernally gay, albeit with a rarefied gaiety in keeping with the rest of the work.

In Salzburg days the opening theme (Ex. 189) would have been a mere refrain, made for sauciness. The constructive and expressive purpose which it serves in this concerto, however, may be seen by looking at a list of extracts showing the various outlets it provides, through principles explained in the opening chapters on concerto structure. Some of these outlets are seen in Exx. 190, 191, and 192, and the extracts following. Ex. 193 comes from the cadenza 'proper', the second cadenza of this movement. Given the same nursery-tune materials, should we have made extensions like that in Ex. 194, or cadenzas of such exact length and brilliance, or put them so exactly in the right places? Should we have hit upon so subtle an imitation of the refrain as that seen in Ex. 196?

Diagrams of Mozart's rondos would show even greater diversity than those of his first movements, for the greater ligamentation makes for more fundamental variety. This last concerto shows Mozart still experimenting, if that is the right word. The sequence of themes is as follows:

1. A–B–A, C, D (in F major), cadenza.
2. A, *bravura* work and concertante writing modulating widely.
3. A, in E flat major.
4. C and D, in tonic key, cadenza.
5. A–B–A.

Each of these sections is joined to the following section by matter which plays with 'A'; thus, by allowing the *full* refrain (A–B–A) only at the beginning and the end, Mozart gives us the usual wealth of subject-matter together with a new integrity of structure.

After the disappointment of the D major Concerto, it is good to think that, in the year of his death, Mozart left us a work which, though omitting the trumpets and drums, is worthy to stand at the end of a great series—in my opinion the greatest series—of works in the most difficult of purely instrumental forms.

CHAPTER XXI

CONCLUSION. MOZART AND MODERN PERFORMANCE

PERFORMANCE: ORCHESTRAL AND SOLO

PERFUNCTORY and over-delicate performances of Mozart are growing rarer, though this age has introduced distortions of its own; sometimes a piece loses entity in its general movement while each section, each phrase, is well preened and pinned; sometimes exaggeration takes an opposite course, and the taut, lithe exquisiteness of Mozart's phrases becomes lost in a tempestuous tribute to his poetry. Archaism and 'historical' preciosity produce rival falsehoods to Schumannizing or Beethovenizing. If prime cuts of Mozart are forced through the machine of this or that school of pianism or of orchestral interpretation, he cannot speak for himself, for we see only the logician, the formalist, the orchestrator, or the poetaster of his time. Under the period surface, Mozart is a chameleon among composers, and maintains a rigid autopsy as soon as we try to superimpose either one colour or one technique; he quivers as soon as we are alertly receptive, so that a clear but firm grasp can let cloud, smile, or grimace, hardness or sentiment, move and pass without emotional slovenliness or alteration of tempo. This is what happens in great Mozart playing when a fine musical intelligence guides a superlative technical mastery instead of trusting to retailed preconceptions. The most lovely moments in great Mozart performances seem the very ones which stress fluidity, so that one recalls Elvira's transition from anger to tenderness, and the memory involuntarily quotes the Whitsun Sequence:

> Flecte quod est rigidum,
> Riga quod est aridum,
> Fove quod est frigidum.

But modern virtuosity is highly specialized. A modest and sincere conductor or player will do well in one concerto or symphony and badly in another; he will seem like the actor Smith, whose Hamlet, Othello, and Teazle were all Smith. This performer, or even the brilliant player who sees the concerto only as so much pianism to be played correctly and exquisitely, is to be preferred to the insolent didactic, who thinks as he manhandles: 'You do not know Mozart; I am now showing you.' Malice dwells lovingly upon Bateman's cartoons of virtuosi, and recognizes various traducers of Mozart—the rigid, the frigid, the soulful, the necrophilistic.

The amateur, with nobody else in his room, hacking out some substitute for the orchestra, keener to know Mozart than to hear himself play, may be the most sensitive and pliable medium in the composer's hands. Transfer him to the concert hall we cannot. A professional of professionals, Mozart demands the virtuoso, with his keen awareness of what is going on around him, and the technical mastery omnipresent even though he become as a little child. Gone are the days, let us hope, when a Mozart concerto was considered fit pabulum for the year's best girl preparing for a terminal concert. There are several fine players who love the Mozart concertos and, so far from despising pianism which comes easily under the hands, being in only two parts for long stretches, regard the invitation to participate in such music as a high honour. Yet not every sincere virtuoso understands the nature of Mozart's pianism, nor the meaning of the word 'participate' when applied to the concertos. Our lack of notable performances comes not from any deliberate egotism, but from the mentality of the average professional executant.

The words 'mere virtuoso' are incongruous and should be contradictory. We rarely hear a recognizable error in public performance, and the reading of a new and difficult score by a standard orchestra astounds the amateur player. The solo virtuoso, like the professional bandsman who can at any moment call himself a solo virtuoso, trains his apprentice to meet all difficulties with the right technique, to be a master at any challenge, *never to make a mistake*, and not to admire vapouring lectures on music in general by critics and choral conductors who cannot say what they mean in terms of instrumental technique. Good players want definite marks upon a copy, precise challenges to their performing skill, and clear instructions at rehearsal; exceptions to this are not always the best players, and it is more important that bandsmen should be reliable virtuosi than that they should be musical scholars, since the dignity or vulgarity of performance is in a conductor's hands. Players do not like their copies littered with extra pencillings, but the conductor may use his own copies whose coloured inkings save breath and patience.

The soloist is very differently placed; he is the guest of honour, and deference is made to his interpretation which some listeners may deplore. On the last two occasions when Beethoven's E flat Concerto was played in London, the soloist did not look at the stick even when synchronization might have been thought essential, e.g.

when a long shake finished with a heavy tonic chord. During works which are virtually sonatas with orchestra, our attention is rightly centred upon the soloist, whom the conductor continually nurses and puts into high relief. But Mozart accentuates the word 'concerto', not 'piano', and the pianist must feel as he does when taking part in trio, quartet, or quintet—that other players are gathered round his instrument because it happens to be large and unportable, and because he is but *primus inter pares*.

The ideal soloist, then, knows himself to be the successor of the continuo-player, and if he is wise he will study from a full score, as did his forebear, and not only from the convenient piano copy. Let him also imagine that the staves are equally spaced on that score and that the notes of the piano part are no heavier than those of other parts; let him indeed recognize his solo position, but let him see the solo part as a line among lines, functional to the texture, contributing to conversation, decorating or completing wind phrases, holding fluid string writing together with its periodic impact of hammer upon string, as well as advancing a movement in one or two places and setting an example to be imitated. In a Mozart concerto the keyboard part differs from that found in other concertos as Mozart's orchestral scoring differs from that of every other composer, and if we grasp the difference in scoring we may hope to understand more clearly the difference in the soloist's functions.

With nearly every other composer, we can examine orchestral scoring as a unit; we can see Brahms's attempt to think of the orchestra as a symphonic whole from which melodic lines have to stand out, and we can compare a two-piano version of his music with its orchestration; we can examine Rimsky-Korsakoff's deliberate choice of certain registers in a group of instruments, and his analysis of the whole orchestral palette into a number of groups and sub-groups, his omission from certain groups of any tone which detracts from maximum luminosity, and his sharp contrasts of one texture with another—pizzicato with arco, double-tongueing with tenuto, brass sforzando with wood pianissimo; we can trace Mahler's wonderful care in achieving balance, until, in the 'Lieder eines fahrenden Gesellen', a huge orchestra accompanies a single voice without incongruity. Yet it will be conceded that most great orchestrators had their conceptions limited, consciously or not, by their instrumental ideals; a Brahms, who writes what is called 'abstract music' in the first place, turns afterwards to the surmounting of definite problems of scoring—balance, colour, variety—and for Mozart such problems do not seem to exist. He may have been lucky; the band may have been at just the right stage of development to make instrumental thinking one element in musical thinking as a whole, just as it is to the modern composer who writes a string quartet.

If Mozart's fortune and not his genius makes his scoring uniquely functional, inseparable from his whole conception, why is not Beethoven's scoring indistinguishable from Mozart's, since he deals with the same orchestra? I am not attempting to think of Beethoven's scoring as 'better' or 'worse' than Mozart's; I merely have in mind that problems of balance and colour are involved in the rehearsal of a Beethoven overture to an extent less obvious with Mozart because of the difference in orchestral texture. A perfunctory studio performance of Mozart does not show its *orchestral* inadequacy so badly as does a similar treatment of Beethoven. Were there difference in size of band, we should not be asking these questions. Schubert, in the great C major Symphony, which he had no opportunity to hear, makes marvellous play with his trombones in the introduction, but he gives conductors some trouble with them afterwards. Against this, we have the glorious memory of Mozart's use of trombones—not, however, as part of any brass 'family', which did not exist as such even in Beethoven's day, even if the list of instrumental staves had trumpets, horns, and trombones.

It seems strange to go as far afield as the 'additional accompaniments' to Handel's oratorios to examine Mozart's scoring in concertos. Yet where else are we to look for any deliberate scoring apart from musical thinking as a whole? I propose, therefore, to use for this purpose what we know to have been *applied* orchestral technique. To study the 'additional accompaniments' is to recognize that they are not merely additional; we may think them impudent indications of what Mozart thought better orchestration than the original. Let us isolate the examples which receive most expressions of disgust from the purists. First I have quoted a passage (Ex. 197) from 'The people that walked in darkness' which some people like to be played tasto solo though we cannot tell what top-dressing it received from Handel's clavecinist. The question is not 'Had Mozart any right to do it?', but 'Does it not make an exquisite whole? Could we add or subtract without spoiling it?' From this let us turn to the music preceding 'The trumpet shall sound' (Ex. 198) which wicked Mozart presumed to foreshorten—to save the trumpeter's lip? To avoid what he thought an otiose and tautologous repetition? We do not know; it does not matter just now. What we can tell, from this or the other

example, or from the brilliant drum and trumpet parts in 'Why do the nations so furiously rage?', is the difference between baroque and rococo scoring. There may be justification for the purist's complaint that baroque music should be scored in the broad baroque manner, and we may note that Mozart himself, in the C minor Mass, the *Requiem*, and the Fantasias for clockwork organ was forced by sheer sense of style to imitate the baroque manner, though he may have had no trace of our modern antiquarian aesthetic.

It is dangerous to use the word 'baroque' too carelessly; musical baroque is a convenient epithet for the broad balance of harmony,

198

mass, and counterpoint, in the age of Bach and Handel. Architectural baroque is by no means a matter of broad masses and lines, and there is little point in pushing the analogy with music. All I seek is a convenient label which musical history fails to provide. The organ is essentially a baroque instrument, the music which suits it best still being that written in broad masses and lines; no modern organ music gives the satisfaction we derive from that of Bach. We learn the instrument chiefly to play Bach, just as choral societies in the north of England foregather chiefly to sing another baroque form—the oratorio chorus—and no modern choruses can quite recapture the Handelian splendour without the conscious imitation which Mozart himself shows. But the older orchestra? No; Mozart thought it barbarous, dull, inelegant, without variety or taste. He shared general contempt for a string body with its bass reinforced by a crowd of bassoons, its treble by a crowd of oboes, its rhythm by the metrical clank of the clavier, its variety by the additional solo trumpet or flute. Rococo taste, with its graceful linear writing, its little quirks for wood-wind, its variety of bowings, rests, its interplay of phrases, its nuances and curves, alternation of more than two dynamic strengths, would 'improve' the old baroque. To us, both conceptions are dated and timeless; there is one glory of the sun and another of the moon, but in Mozart's 'improvements' we see what we cannot improve, though we may scrap them altogether, and play what we imagine to be Handel.

In the additional accompaniments, we can at least observe the rococo ideal of scoring; but when the scoring is part and parcel of Mozart's rococo music, we cannot see the grain without seeing the wood itself; we can only point to places where wood and its graining are simultaneously shapely. He who would write a treatise upon Mozart and the orchestra can but fill his text with musical quotations, stand aside from them, and become a showman. Some such quotations are made in the pages of this study, but a single miniature score will reveal the all and the nothing one could teach a composition student about Mozartian instrumental felicity. Let one point illustrate the difficulty of the task. In another composer, one would look for problems of balance and colour in the heaviest parts of a score; but it is precisely in the tempestuous concertos that Mozart puts most burden upon the strings; their syncopations, sforzandi, tremolo bowings, and sudden silences give character to the works; the beautiful curves and rococo ornaments, the pathetically sustained chords, the little dialogues with the solo—these things which are complementary to the powerful string writing are the function of wind instruments; but they are sublimely essential. Omit a clarinet or a flute and there is a blank space in the sound, as if an explosion had brought down a cornice in a city church, or the wainscot in a guild hall.

The solo is but the most important of these instrumental lines, as it is also partner in the whole concerto conception. Its first task, then, is a simple one—always to be present and correct; but this cannot invariably be found among soloists. Elsewhere I have spoken of the opening solo in the D minor Concerto (see Ex. 4). Unless its first three crotchets fall in exactly the tempo set by the orchestra, the concerto conception is mocked. The egotism which so often makes a short rest between prelude and first hammer-fall says plainly: 'I begin here; that had nothing to do with me'—but each *has* everything to do with the other, and one participant has no meaning without the other. Could a flute or an oboe, finding its part technically easy, take similar liberty? How many pianists, nay, how many conductors, can achieve either strict tempo or clear articulation with such a Mozartian commonplace as Ex. 97c—a rhythm which opens at

least four concertos? How many still turn 2/4 ♩. ♪ ♩ into 6/8 ♩ ♪ ♩. or 2/4 ♪ ♪ ♩? Bandsmen and soloists are frequently carried away in passages which provide a long chain of notes with similar duration;

one recalls a fine pianist who drew the blood up Sir Thomas Beecham's neck by rushing the left hand triplets in K. 453, thus taking the perkiness out of the 'starling' tune. As for the use of rubato, Mozart's own words have been quoted, but one must acknowledge the difference between artistic interpretations which are impelled to bend tempo to a fine purpose, and vagaries which come from lack of control and emotional vulgarity. Whole passages of the concertos may best be treated with absolute periodicity of tempo, or an attempt at it which will be in no danger of making the soloist into an automaton.

In the past few years, isolated performances, one or two happily recorded, have been in charge of a great musician or of two great musicians in league and of one mind. This is sincere homage to Mozart. Many of the few broadcast performances, both in this country and elsewhere, show a lingering of perfunctory and misguided condescension; the scales, arpeggios, and pedalling may be easy after playing Tchaikovsky and Rachmaninoff; but the intelligence Mozart demands is more than can be bestowed by study of pianism or by musical scholarship. Even deep scholarship is not enough. The romantic interpretation errs no more than does that which drags in a harpsichord and accepts all other modern media, including the score; intelligent scholarship, however, reduces the battery of cellos and basses, together with the mass of violin tone which swamps the wind delineations more than it does the percussive solo. Antiquarian aesthetic may prevent us giving Mozart the cavalier treatment he gave Handel; we have no musical parallels to 'Shakespeare in modern dress'. To put candles on the desks, issue wigs and cravats, provide a harpsichord, and yet regard Breitkopf and Härtel as sacrosanct, is to give ourselves an interesting and jolly evening's entertainment, no more to be confused with accurate Mozart-playing than a recent and interesting reading of *Twelfth Night* by phoneticians was to be confused with 'Shakespeare as he wrote it'.

The playing of a long and inept cadenza is not so offensive as the mishandling of a whole concerto, and there is some excuse for ignorance of the function of cadenzas in the earlier type of concerto. The cadenzas of virtuoso composers in the nineteenth century were climactic, drawing yet more from materials which were few in number and used in each section—exposition, development, and recapitulation. Brilliance and invention were rightly stretched to the utmost, and such cadenzas as that in Schumann's Concerto are glorious things which cannot be called mere decorations to the movement or improvisations for the soloist. It must be stressed in regard to Mozart's

6

cadenzas, not so much that they are but embellishments—protracted cadences—like those made by singers in arias of the period, but that to intrude something highly organized and climactic into a highly organized movement is to nurture a weeping tumour. All too frequently we console ourselves with the thought that, since the movement is almost finished, we have heard Mozart and are aware of his general design, so that we can settle down to ten minutes of Hummel, Tausig, Reinecke, or Sekles.[1] Mozart's own cadenzas should be played where they are available, and should be models when they are not available; they are slight, often brilliant, and usually, though not invariably, make reference to a theme or themes. There is never any elaborate counterpoint or structure, and the theme chosen for a starting-point is rarely the chief one, or one which has been played in the preceding ritornello. One quality is invariable—brevity (see opposite).

It may be remarked that I have said nothing about (a) ornaments in performance, or (b) the soloist's occasional or permanent function as continuo or thoroughbass player. These are still matters to be debated by textual scholars, but they *are* still debatable and also, so far as the performer is concerned, of small importance. That it was still customary for the soloist to provide continuo when Beethoven produced his C major Concerto the student will find by consulting the Eulenburg score of that work, edited by W. Altmann, but I should think him a pedant if he aired his knowledge of the matter when performing the work, or when performing a mature Mozart concerto with orchestras of the usual modern size as his partners. We can enter into the musical world of Mozart without the aid of singer or player who, in the matter of ornaments, tries to reproduce the practices of Mozart's day. The last attempt to perform *Messiah* as Handel wrote it was a failure; it is impossible, in the first place, to achieve such a feat; in the second place the attempt was inartistic by normal musical standards. It included an appoggiatura on 'know' in 'I know that my Redeemer liveth'.

Because it is not the purpose of this book to deal with textual matters let it not be supposed that textual scholarship is despised. A great deal may be learnt even by comparing Blume's edition of concertos in the Eulenburg edition with the former Breitkopf and

[1] Very few would wish to see the Beethoven cadenzas to the D minor Concerto abandoned. They cannot be said to show inordinate length or stylistic incongruity, and they seem to be a sincere and modest attempt to avoid such incongruity. The chief trouble is that a rival turn of genius cannot help just showing itself—in other words, Beethoven's cadenzas are too interesting.

Härtel text which we have usually played at concerts, and it is to be hoped that the Eulenberg editions will soon be completed, to be as valuable in their department as are the Einstein editions of the Mozart quartets. Even when debatable and unimportant to the performer, textual opinions are valuable, and their minutiae may prove as valuable as their main theses in the light of subsequent research. In this respect musical research does not differ from research in other sciences; schoolboys thought the study of electrostatics to be a mere academic necessity before the age of radio.

If these notes, with their frequent digressions, send readers to scores and make either performers or public of the next generation take a fresh interest in these beautiful works, I shall feel that my writing was more than a pleasure for the writer.

CONCERTOS WITH MOZART'S CADENZAS AVAILABLE

K. 175 in D	Movt. 1 and 2. Two versions of each cadenza.
K. 246 in C	Movt. 1, two cadenzas. Movt. 2, three cadenzas.
K. 271 in E flat	Two cadenzas available for each movement.
K. 365 in E flat (Two pianos)	Cadenzas to Movts. 1 and 3.
K. 382	Supplementary rondo to K. 175.
K. 413 in F	Cadenzas to Movts. 1 and 2.
K. 414 in A	Cadenzas to all movements, two for Movt. 2.
K. 415 in C	Cadenzas to all movements.
K. 449 in E flat	Cadenza to Movt. 1.
K. 450 in B flat	Cadenzas to Movts. 1 and 3.
K. 451 in D	Cadenzas to Movts. 1 and 3.
K. 453 in G	Cadenzas to Movts. 1 and 2. Two sets.
K. 456 in B flat	Two cadenzas to Movt. 1. One cadenza to Movt. 3.
K. 459 in F	Cadenzas to Movts. 1 and 3.
K. 488 in A	Cadenza to Movt. 1.
K. 595 in B flat	Cadenzas to Movts. 1 and 3.

A thematic guide to the cadenzas will be found under Section 624 of Alfred Einstein's edition of Köchel's catalogue. The whole series has been recently issued, however, in a good edition by Broude Bros. of New York.

INDEX